Gathering Empty Pitchers

Faith Writings Volume III
Alisa Hope Wagner

Marked Writers Publishing

Gathering Empty Pitchers

Faith Writings Volume III

Gathering Empty Pitchers
Faith Writings For a Mother's Soul
Faith Writings Volume III
Short story illustration by Albert Morales
Copyright @ 2015 by Alisa Hope Wagner
Marked Writers Publishing
www.alisahopewagner.com

Scriptures taken from various Bible translations.

Author photo by Monica Lugo
Edits by Faith Newton

ISBN-13: 978-0692415887
ISBN-10: 0692415882
BISAC: Devotional / Christian / Religious/ Nonfiction

Dedication

God, my Creator, my Savior, my Counselor

Daniel, my high school sweetheart and soul mate

Isaac, my firstborn son

Levi, my brown-eyed boy

Karis Ruth, my cherished girl

Christina, my twin and my friend

Forward

This collection of faith writings is book 3 of the Vessels Series written over a ten-year span. When a life is given over to God's care, a slow transformation begins to take place. It is difficult to explain this change in a bullet list of conclusions. However, the "ever-increasing" transformation can be experienced in real-life stories. That's what this book represents—a glimpse into the heart of an imperfect person in love with a perfect God.

"And we all, who with unveiled faces contemplate the Lord's glory, are being transformed into his image with ever-increasing glory, which comes from the Lord, who is the Spirit" (2 Corinthians 3.18 NIV).

Vessels Series

Imperfect Vessels
Broken Alabaster Jars
Gathering Empty Pitchers

Gathering Empty Pitchers

Women are constantly serving the needs of others. Almost every night we fall into our beds depleted of energy and devoid of passion. We are completely empty, and we wonder how we'll find the strength to make it through another day.

I've had many nights like this. Out of obedience, I pour into the lives of family and friends, and I fulfill the many obligations that come with life. Hands continuously grope at the fleeting seconds of my day, and I desperately search for the scraps. When there are no leftovers to be found, I hold my empty hands up to God and cry out, "Lord, there is nothing left for me!"

As I contemplated more ways to hoard my little scraps, God taught me a beautiful lesson that has forever changed my life. He taught me how to Gather Empty Pitchers!

I read the story about Elisha and the widow found in 2 Kings. 4.1-7.

A prophet died and left his wife and sons with a considerable debt. The debtor was going to come and take the widow's sons away to pay for the debt. The widow came to Elisha and asked for his help.

Elisha asked the woman if she had anything of value, and at first the woman said no; but then she admitted to having a little oil.

Elisha told the woman to gather all the pitchers she could find and take the oil and fill each of them. The oil poured out until there were no more empty pitchers. The woman was able to sell the oil and keep her sons.

When I read this story, I imagined the woman carefully pouring her oil into each pitcher. As she held one of the pitchers and poured oil to its rim, she cried out, "Another pitcher, please!" But there were no more. I could see the desperation on the woman's face as she realized how very few pitchers she had filled.

I felt the woman's anguish over not having more pitchers. I wished that she would have been more prepared. If she would have taken Elisha's words more seriously, she would have spent weeks or even months gathering empty pitchers. That's when I felt God say to me, "You are gathering empty pitchers."

I didn't quite understand what God meant, but I knew He was about to give me hope in my obedient emptiness.

I meditated on the story for several days, discussing it with God and friends. Finally, I felt the last puzzle piece fall into place and an amazing image of empty pitchers appeared in my mind. I figured out how I could gather empty pitchers! At long last, I understood how I could find my "true self" by sacrificing myself!

Jesus said, "Anyone who intends to come with me has to let me lead. You're not in the driver's seat—I am. Don't run from suffering; embrace it. Follow me and I'll show you how. Self-help is no help at all. Self-sacrifice is the way, my way, to finding yourself, your true self. What good would it do to get everything you want and lose you, the real you?" (Luke 9.23 MSG).

How could "Self-sacrifice" be beneficial to finding my "true self"?

If God is my Creator and the Creator of all things, wouldn't it stand to reason that He knows me better than I know myself? And if He designed me for a specific purpose, wouldn't it be to my benefit that I surrender to His will completely?

But why does it seem that God would have us continuously pour ourselves into those around us? So many times we want to be like the widow. She didn't want to let Elisha know that she had a small jar of oil at home. We do the same thing. We don't want to let go of the little time, resources and energy we have because we're scared there will be nothing left for us.

But this is not the case. Every time we pour our lives out for God's glory, we leave an empty pitcher for God to fill. Every time we serve the needs of our children, we leave an empty pitcher. Every time we sacrifice our bodies for our husbands, we leave an empty pitcher.

Every time we pour into the lives of our friends, we leave an empty pitcher. Every time we give resources to the poor and disadvantaged, we leave an empty pitcher. And every time we surrender our desires to the Holy Spirit, we leave an empty pitcher.

Sometimes God fills those empty pitchers immediately, and we are instantly blessed for our sacrifice. However, most of the time, the empty pitchers gather. God allows them to gather because He knows that He is about to open the heavens and pour down the blessings. He wants you to be ready with a bunch of empty pitchers, so you do not cry out, "Another pitcher, please!"

This revelation has helped me because now I look forward to leaving empty pitchers. Every time I serve those around me, I open myself to be blessed by God. And the most awesome part about pouring myself out to others is that God loves my emptiness! He can complete His divine work only in my emptiness! The "real me" shows up when I have nothing left to hoard!

Be constantly mindful, though, that you do not try to get others to fill your pitchers. Wait on God's hand! If we expect others to give us something in return, God will not bless our actions. He only fills empty pitchers (Matthew 6.1).

Sometimes we forget that God is the everlasting Creator. He specializes in creating something out of nothing. In the Old Testament, God created life out of emptiness: "Now the earth was formless and empty, darkness was over the surface of the deep, and the Spirit of God was hovering over the waters" (Genesis 1.2 NIV). And in the New Testament, God created new life from an Empty Tomb (John 20).

If we are constantly pouring ourselves into the lives of others, God is able to create something beautiful within our emptiness. So many times we think we could do a better job than God can at molding us. We pray to God to make us more like Him; then, we scold Him for not doing things our way (Isaiah 29.16). God created life! How could we possibly top that? Whenever we try to take control, we just create chaos and heartache.

God in His infinite wisdom knows that we want to meddle with His creation, so He ensures our humility by keeping us continually poured out to others. Our brokenness allows the Holy Spirit to easily pour through us, and it makes us more malleable so that God can complete the good work He started in us (Philippians 1.6).

God is so awesome because He made our self-sacrifice doubly good. God blesses us when we sacrifice for others because we are able to leave empty pitchers for Him to fill, and He blesses us when we sacrifice for others because He is able to create us into His image.

It's the best two-for-one-deal in the entire universe! This is why

Jesus said that the only way to find your "true self" is to sacrifice yourself. Only God knows our "true self" and only He can complete His design.

So the next time you feel exhausted and your lift your empty hands up to God, cry out to Him, "God, create life in me!" And if you feel like you've messed up the life He has already given you, lift up your hands to Him and cry out, "God, create new life in me!"

If you can stay broken by continually pouring yourself into the lives of others, God will be able to bless you and create your emptiness into a thing of beauty. Don't hold anything back! Trust God with all you have and start gathering empty pitchers!

Both Eyes Open

"There are also heavenly bodies and there are earthly bodies; but the splendor of the heavenly bodies is one kind, and the splendor of the earthly bodies is another" (1 Corinthians 15.40 NIV).

I couldn't help but stare at my daughter. We were in the backyard, letting our new puppy run and play. My baby girl's expression was animated with amusement as she watched the brown, miniature dachshund chase her pink princess ball. The morning was bright and sunny, but I made sure that we each wore hooded jackets to protect our faces from the crisp, cool wind.

I sat in a wicker chair, thankful that both my daughter and the puppy burned a ton of their childish energy during their play. My daughter continually kicked the pink ball and cried with delight when he went to chase it. I knew they would be tuckered out soon, and I could foresee long naps in their distant future. I felt so blessed, like God had written, casted and directed a mini-movie just for my pleasure.

As I watched my girl, I noticed that something happened to my view. I could see her playing, but I could also see a white covering blocking my view. I finally realized that the hood of my jacket had fallen over my right eye. When I stared at her, I could see both the presence and absence of her simultaneously.

I squinted my right eye, and I could see my daughter clearly through my left eye. Then, I squinted my right eye, and my daughter disappeared behind the curtain of my hood. I opened both eyes, and my vision was filled with her presence again, yet the corner of my hood still blocked half my view.

"Maybe I should just keep my right eye closed," I said to myself.

"But I gave you two eyes," the Holy Spirit whispered back.

Just like Jesus, we are people born of two worlds: our outer person was born of the physical world, but our inner person was born of a spiritual world. When our inner person is brought to life through Christ, we will see life through both sets of eyes; and God has designed our view to incorporate both worlds. The question is, which eye will be our dominate eye?

God makes many promises in the Bible, and the Holy Spirit gives us many promises individually. However, it is hard to chase those promises when we don't see them. Many times our spiritual eye is weak because we've allowed our physical eye to dominate our lives. But when we practice cultivating our spiritual eye through deepening our relationship with Christ, reading the Bible and trusting the leading of the Holy Spirit, our spiritual eye begins to awaken.

The point isn't learning how to shut out the physical view; rather, it's learning to see through both eyes and give precedence to our spiritual view. Seeing both the presence of God's miracles (in the spiritual realm) and the absence of God's miracles (in the physical realm) simultaneously, forces us to walk by faith. And chasing after these promises forces us to strengthen our spiritual eye and give it dominance over our lives.

The Bible says, "The heavens belong to the LORD, but he has given the earth to all humanity" (Psalm 115.16 NLT). Although God is the creator and controller over the universe, He gives His children, humankind, free will to create good on the earth. It's up to us to look through both our physical and spiritual eye, pluck out those spiritual promises and transplant them into reality on this earth.

We need both eyes open to accomplish our purpose in this life, but we must always remember to trust our spiritual eye most. Only the spiritual eye can tap into the presence, abundance, love and mercy of the Lord. The physical eye allows us to see the blank slate on which God wants us to create our best lives.

Direct Path of Light

"Therefore do not become partners with them; for at one time you were darkness, but now you are light in the Lord. Walk as children of light" (Ephesians 5.7-8 ESV).

My husband and I recently added a puppy to our family of five. Now that our kids are all potty trained, I finally relented to the extra duties involved with caring for a pet. Needless to say, our kids were ecstatic to meet our new family member, and he has become the mascot of our household.

Just like babies, puppies need to be potty trained. After months of accidents in the house, I decided that our little puppy was finally getting it. However, I wasn't sure if he was being trained to potty outside or if we were being trained to constantly walk him. Either way, we have all learned to adjust to the changes of our growing family.

My husband usually walks him at night before we go to bed, and I usually walk him early in the morning before the sun rises. During both walks, we have to bring a flashlight or we can't see in the dark surrounding us. I keep the light on the puppy's path, so he can see where he is going, and so I can know when he's finished and we can head back inside.

The flashlight is one of those outdoor camping lights that give off a very bright beam. When pointed directly ahead, it can light up the entire path. I remember walking our puppy one morning in awe of how much light penetrated the darkness of our yard with the flashlight. But when I pointed the flashlight straight up into the dark sky, the light vanished—it was swallowed up by the black abyss. It was only effective when used in the forefront of where we walked.

As I stared at the shadowy depths of the sky where my light disappeared, the Holy Spirit whispered a powerful truth to me. He said that many of us waste our lights trying to point them in the wrong direction. Instead of pointing our lights unapologetically where God has planted us, we aim them in places where we haven't been called. And we wonder in despair why we are not effective at shining God's light to the world.

Sometimes we are guided by a misconception that we have to penetrate a wide chasm with our lights in order for our ministries, lives and words to be meaningful. But that is just not true. Jesus told his disciples to look around them. The harvest is everywhere, but the workers are few (Matthew 9.37-38). God has placed us right where He needs us, and He will light our paths to where we need to go (Psalm 119.105). Pointing our lights in any other direction other than the one God is leading us would be a waste of our talents, time and energy.

So instead of feeling anxiety about trying to pierce a sea of unknown darkness, I can find satisfaction and purpose when I allow the Holy Spirit to spread His light through my life in the domain in which He has appointed me. I can share the hope I find in Jesus to those faces who cross my path and to those beautiful souls He has entrusted to my care. I have a lot of light to give, and I want to make sure every ounce of my God-given luminous intensity makes a difference.

"No one lights a lamp and then hides it or puts it under a basket. Instead, a lamp is placed on a stand, where its light can be seen by all who enter the house" (Luke 11.33 NLT).

Marriage

Today is my 15th wedding anniversary with my husband! We met at 16, started dating at 17 and married at 22. Now at 37, I can honestly say that my marriage is my most favorite aspect of life besides my relationship with God through Jesus Christ.

I've always heard people ask the question, "What is the one thing that makes your marriage work?"

And I've contemplated it through the years. I've come up with different answers, but I believe there is one key that helps a marriage not only work, but flourish. I don't confess to be a marriage expert (if there is such a thing), but I can say that I truly love and enjoy being united with my husband.

The key that I've learned may sound simple, but the beauty and benefits of it will absolutely change a marriage. Not only does it bless the couple as a whole, but it quiets all the individual straining and yearning that put spouses at odds. Mainly, my conclusion is this: In a marriage, the individual dies so the marriage can thrive.

Well meaning people will say to put all your spouse's needs above your own, but I would disagree. A marriage consists of two parts: a woman and a man and focusing on one person is lopsided and will hinder the marriage. Therefore, for a marriage to prosper, the wants and needs of both people must be considered. As a wife, I can objectively look at my marriage in any given situation and make decisions based on what would be best for the marriage as a whole. Sometimes that means that I highlight my need; sometimes that means that I highlight my husband's need.

A woman and a man bring equal value into a marriage. The man has strengths, weaknesses, wants and desires, as does the woman. And when we speak the words, "I do," the journey of becoming truly one begins. As the years go by, the individual lines begin to blur and an amazing oneness starts to form. The needs of one become the needs of both, and peace and joy permeate the relationship. I am happy when my husband's needs are met because his needs have become my needs and vice versa.

I am still who God created me to be, but the essence of who I am has merged with another uniquely designed person. Much like an egg and a sperm, we spiritually, emotional and physically become one. "Me" has become "Us," so together we can live for "Him." This doesn't mean that we lose our individual personalities (my husband can attest to that), but it does mean that our personality is half of a greater "marriage personality."

Finally, when we each keep our eyes on Jesus, the combining of two lives becomes much easier. Jesus and His Word with the refining power of the Holy Spirit give us a path of Truth. When my husband and I follow in that Truth, we will both walk in the right direction together. It doesn't mean we won't have arguments or frustrations—especially during difficult times—but it does mean that we willingly choose to continue to love each other and to die to self so our marriage can prosper.

"For this reason a man shall leave [behind] his father and his mother and be joined to his wife and cleave closely to her permanently, and the two shall become one flesh, so that they are no longer two, but one flesh. What therefore God has united (joined together), let not man separate or divide" (Mark 10.7-9 AMP).

The Gift of Gratitude

"Be thankful in all circumstances, for this is God's will for you who belong to Christ Jesus" (1 Thessalonians 5.18 NLT).

I took my five-year-old daughter grocery shopping. She had been such a trooper that day, coming with me on all my errands that I wanted to bless her with a gift. Ever since my daughter was just a toddler, it was obvious to all of us that her love language was gifts. She loves receiving presents! I decided to let her pick out a small present from the toy section at the store to bless her.

My daughter has trouble choosing what she wants. Every toy looks amazing to her, and she gets torn between which special item she wants to choose. On this particular day, there were two toys that she wanted. I explained that we had to leave before my frozen items began to melt, so she finally had to choose one.

On the way home, as she clung to her new blessing, all she could talk about was the toy that she didn't get. She whined and complained our entire drive. I almost wished that I hadn't blessed her in the first place because of all the grief it caused her! Finally, when we made it to our house, I knew that I needed to talk with her about gratitude.

"Are you happy with the toy that I bought you?" I asked.

"Yes," she said, nodding her head.

"Well, I haven't heard you say 'Thank you' yet, and you don't seem excited or happy about your new toy."

She held her gift tightly in her hands.

"When someone gives you a blessing, they feel good inside. And when you are super excited and show gratitude, it makes them want to do it again."

I could tell she was listening intently—she was discovering the secret to receiving more gifts! "Have you shown me any gratitude for this blessing?"

She shook her head no.

"Will I want to buy you another gift if all you did for this gift was complain and whine?"

"I don't know," she answered.

"I want you to focus on the wonderful present in your hands and not the other toy at the store. When you show gratefulness, people will feel good about blessing you and they will want to do it again!"

She nodded in agreement and smiled. I was glad we had our little life lesson together.

My daughter's attitude reminded me of times in my past when I took God's blessings for granted, and I lacked gratitude. I was so consumed with what He hadn't given me yet that I didn't see all the blessings that I already had in my life! God blesses me daily with family, friendships, health, purpose etc., and I want to show Him how excited and grateful I am that He would think about me.

More importantly, I am saved from an eternity separated from God because of Jesus' finished work on the cross. I want to thank Jesus every day for my salvation. Yes, this life can be painful and we have to endure hardships, but our redemption is secure in Christ.

I have a covenant relationship with a holy God that will last forever because Jesus sealed my forgiveness with His blood. I should be waking up every morning filled with gratitude and joy that I will live for eternity with God in heaven

"My Father, who has given them to me, is greater than all; no one can snatch them out of my Father's hand" (John 10.29 NIV).

Dog Biscuits

My dachshund, Rusty, is a dog food snob. He would rather beg table scraps or chomp down dog biscuits than eat his healthy, tailored made dog food. One morning before leaving the house, I wanted to give Rusty a couple of his favorite dog biscuits. However, it was a cold day, so he was upstairs in our bed, snuggled up under the covers.

I decided to leave him his favorite snacks downstairs, so when hunger and thirst forced him out of his comfortable slumber, he would have the biscuits waiting for him. I placed his two delicious treats in his dog dish—right on top of his usually ignored dog food. I stared at the two biscuits for a moment and wondered how surprised he would be to find his favorite food on top of the food he begrudgingly ate!

Several hours later, I came home. Rusty greeted me at the door, and I went straight to his dog dish to see if he found his special surprise. When I walked to his dish, I saw his two delicious treats just sitting there uneaten! He never found the biscuits I gave him because he ignored the food that we regularly provided for him.

And I wondered how often Christians ignore the special surprises God has for us in the areas of our lives that we take most for granted. We complain about doing dishes, yet we are blessed to have food to eat and dishes to eat on! We complain about folding laundry, yet we are blessed to have clothes on our back that not only protect us, but make us feel and look good. We complain about our jobs, yet we are blessed to earn a living in order to provide for our families and contribute to society! And this list goes on and on.

Maybe we've taken for granted the abundance for which God has placed in front of us, and we miss the small treats that He puts in our path. I have discovered that the truly beautiful blessings in my life are found in the normal, everyday moments of my day. I help one of my kids with homework, and I'm gifted a beautiful smile of a child who loves me. I cook dinner for my family, and I'm gifted the satisfaction of filling the bellies of my loved ones. I encourage my husband's dreams, and I'm gifted with a man who speaks affirmation into my life.

I'm determined not to take God's provision in my life for granted. And I will be on the lookout for the small surprises He gives me throughout my day.

"And whatever you do, whether in word or deed, do it all in the name of the Lord Jesus, giving thanks to God the Father through him" (Colossians 3.17 NIV).

Two Trips

We moved the day before we took our family to Disneyland. Call us crazy, but we filled our home with boxes and caught a plane the next morning to California. As the movers carried the large furniture pieces into our home the evening before our trip, I thought I would help by scooting one of the dressers out of the way. Little did I know how sore I would be the next day...and the next...and the day after...and the day after that...

I had somehow infuriated a nerve that began right under my left ear, ran down my right shoulder and stopped at my fingertips. I had never felt so much continuous pain before. I was in pain on the airplane, at the condo and, sadly, at Disneyland (and a week after we came home). I couldn't even turn my head without pivoting my entire body.

Something similar to this happened to me when I went skiing in Colorado a few months before. We got to the ski resort, and I had finally made it up on my first mountain on the first day of our ski trip, and WHAM! I got slammed by a snowboarder right on my quadriceps. I skied down the hour-long track in pain, and I had to sit out the rest of the trip. In my mind, the ski trip was ruined.

However, the difference between my ski trip and my Disney trip was my attitude. During the ski trip, I was upset, and it showed. I was angry that I couldn't ski, and my attitude teetered to the dark side. When I finally left for home, I was struck with the fact that I had harbored a negative attitude. The memories of my attitude were way more memorable then the memories of the trip itself, and I vowed never to let my attitude sink to that level again. I would put my expectations aside and enjoy the day that God had given me.

So at Disneyland, I realized that I would not be able to do any of the fast and exciting rollercoaster rides that I was anticipating. For months, I had looked forward to enjoying all that the theme park had to offer, but I knew that my injury would worsen with even the slightest jerk or turn. Instead of allowing my attitude to turn for the worst, though, I embraced the change in my plans. I kept my five-year-old daughter with me the entire time, and we enjoyed calm Disney rides, fun shows and the exciting parades.

When I arrived home after this trip, I was left with amazing memories and the knowledge that I had made the best of my situation. My joy was not dependent on my circumstance, and I embraced how blessed I was to even be there. At the end of our lives, I think what will shine the most will not be what we experienced but how we reacted to those experiences. I want to live my life with the joy of the Lord always being the end result of my struggles, heartache and pain.

"This is the day that the LORD has made; We will rejoice and be glad in it" (Psalm 118.24 NKJV).

The Pink Butterfly

I was zipping up my five-year-old daughter's pink jacket, and I noticed that the zipper was a cute pink butterfly. "Oh!" I exclaimed. "Your zipper has little butterfly. How sweet!"

My daughter sighed and replied, "I know, Mommy. I saw that a long time ago."

And Jesus' words about the little children hit me square in the nose: "Let the little children come to me, and do not hinder them, for the kingdom of heaven belongs to such as these" (Matthew 19.14 NIV).

I'm realizing that I'm missing a lot of the precious details of my everyday life–the same details that incorporate God's amazing Kingdom on this earth. I'm rushing so much that the beautiful, little things surrounding me go unnoticed by my eyes and unmoved by my heart. My daughter notices these small, pretty things because she, like most children, is living in the here and now. Her mind isn't off on a million different things that she needs to be doing.

The sad part about this story is that I bought her the pink jacket last spring on sale. I've been holding it for almost nine months, and I have been zipping the same jacket on her for several weeks now, and I just noticed that cute detail. How much more have I missed of God's amazing creation because I'm too busy to notice?

I have realized that I need to slow down. I only want to focus on what I need to accomplish this day only because I want to do my best to experience all that God has blessed me with each day. I'm tired of living in the future, missing all the sweet details of the present. I want my eyes to be like my little girl's eyes. Everything in God's precious Kingdom belongs to her because she sees and absorbs every detail of its beauty.

"Therefore do not worry about tomorrow, for tomorrow will worry about itself. Each day has enough trouble of its own" (Matthew 6.34 NIV).

Connecting Faith

I let my kids play on my phone sometimes. I'm vaguely aware of the few games that I've downloaded. I know they are learning games that keep them challenged. Today, we began our family vacation for Spring Break, and I found myself bored on my flight. So I decided to look at what games were on my phone to see if any of them were interesting enough to pass the time.

I found one that I didn't quite understand at first. Several color-coded dots were displayed on the screen in some sort of diagram, and I was supposed to connect the matching colored dots in lines without crisscrossing on the colored connections. At first, the connections were easy, and I was able to completely fill up the diagram with my connections. However, as I continued to accelerate through the levels, I found the connections harder and harder to make.

Finally, I was stuck at a level. Since I had no experience with the game, I thought some of the levels were tricks—meaning that adequate connections were impossible. I was going to give up, but I decided to show my 10-year old son to make sure I had a valid reason to end the game. He quickly took my phone, made the connections and advanced to the next level.

I realized that every level had an answer. There was ALWAYS a way to beat the game. When I gained this understanding, the levels were easier for me to advance through. I knew that somehow, someway I would find the answer and win. This knowledge forced me to make connections that were wiggly and roundabout. Many times I would have to try over and over again, looking for the right path. The harder the level, the longer it took me to figure out the path to win, but I patiently waited until the answer would finally come to me.

This reminds me a lot of faith. Sometimes a situation looks impossible, but if God says that we can do it, we must look for a way. This may mean that we do things that don't seem natural to us or that exist outside the world's standard, but we must trust that God sees the answer, and He's wanting us to stretch our understanding and build our faith to find it. We can't lose heart or give up. If God says there's a way, there IS a way—even if it is squiggly and roundabout! We can activate our faith in the impossible situations, knowing that through God and the power of Jesus Christ, nothing is ever impossible!

"Jesus looked at them and said, 'With man this is impossible, but with God all things are possible'" (Matthew 19.26 NIV).

The Joy of Losing Weight

I've been thinking about the amount of work it takes to lose and maintain weight. After having each of my three babies, I had to lose 25 plus pounds. It took me about a year of hard work and self-discipline to get back into shape.

Even maintaining weight as I'm doing now takes constant vigilance, and I become overwhelmed sometimes with all the work life on this earth creates. We work at our health, relationships, careers, homes and even our salvation—going from glory to glory into the image of Christ (2 Corinthians 3.18). Paul says in Philippians 2.12-13 that we should do this work without grumbling:

"Therefore, my dear friends, as you have always obeyed—not only in my presence, but now much more in my absence—continue to work out your salvation with fear and trembling, for it is God who works in you to will and to act in order to fulfill his good purpose. Do everything without grumbling or arguing..." (NIV).

But I do find myself grumbling. I realize, though, if I grumbled about all the work I had to do, I would be grumbling all the time. And if I carried a negative attitude about all my work, I would try to consume more distractions—shopping, eating, entertaining, etc.—in order to feel better about life. However, my negative attitude would eventually spread like cancer to all areas of my life if I allowed it to persist.

I can't simply consume to make myself happy because Jesus has called me to work and a purpose (Ephesians 1.11). Jesus says that our lives on this earth are about serving, not simply receiving:

"And he sat down and called the twelve. And he said to them, 'If anyone would be first, he must be last of all and servant of all'" (Mark 9.35 ESV).

Since I'm called to serve, the answer to my "work" dilemma is my heart. I can choose to have a good attitude or a bad attitude. I can choose to grumble about my work or I can see it as an honor. The Bible says to "take captive every thought to make it obedient to Christ" (2 Corinthians 10.5 NIV).

I know that Jesus wants me to be hopeful in all my thoughts (Psalm 31.24). I know that my negative thoughts can start to affect every area of my life, including my health (Proverbs 17.22). I know that Jesus came to this earth to set me free from darkness (Ephesians 5.8). Finally, I know that God has called me to be joyful (1 Thessalonians 5.16) and that His joy in me is my strength (Nehemiah 8.10).

So I understand that if I can work at making my thoughts more positive—even when it feels fake or forced at first—that I will begin to produce positive thoughts in all areas of my life, and my grumbling would be destroyed. I can claim joy when I exercise, do laundry, skip dessert, write, cook for my family, serve a friend, etc. And when I look back on my life, I might not remember everything I did, but I will remember that my attitude was pleasing to the Lord.

"So I saw that there is nothing better for people than to be happy in their work. That is our lot in life. And no one can bring us back to see what happens after we die" (Ecclesiastes 3.22 NLT).

The Forgotten Groceries

I went grocery shopping for a few items, and I when I put my car into park on the driveway, I did what is very typical of me: I tried to carry every single grocery bag into my house in one trip. Since my hands were both draped with bags of heavy groceries, I was unable to close the car door. From the start, I knew I would eventually have to make a trip back to close it.

Once I made it to my front porch, I had to set down some bags so I could unlock and open the door. Finally, when I made it into the house, I had to flex every single one of my arm muscles in order to set the groceries on the kitchen counter. As I walked outside to close the car door, I noticed that I had left a bag behind. Good thing I couldn't close the car door, I thought. I would have spoiled that bag of groceries.

But God knew that I left a bag behind, so He made sure that I would have to make another trip.

I think so many times women become caught up in this trap of trying to do everything at once. We want to be good mothers, wives, influential Christians who have stellar careers, and we want to do it all at the same time. However, when we try to do everything in one trip, we inevitably leave something behind. God will lead us back on another trip to see what we have forgotten.

We may find ourselves too busy to help a friend in need, too drained to adequately care for our families, or too distracted to find rest in the Lord. We are so occupied with trying to achieve our goals all at once that we are no longer enjoying the journey. And we wonder why every night we fall into bed exhausted and discouraged.

God has given us many passions and promises, but He doesn't expect us to achieve them all at the same time. There is a time and a season for everything. If we were to break our goals into several life trips—instead of trying to carry all our dreams at once—we wouldn't leave things behind. We would also find that our load every day is lighter and easier to bear, and that each day we have adequate time to spend in the presence of our Lord.

"Take my yoke upon you. Let me teach you, because I am humble and gentle at heart, and you will find rest for your souls. For my yoke is easy to bear, and the burden I give you is light" (Matthew 11.29-30 NLT).

Using Our Filters

When my husband and I were first married, we lived in a tiny apartment. I could vacuum the entire house using one plug for the cord. My mom came to visit for a few days. She didn't mind sleeping on the couch, but she did mind the lack of coffee supplies. She quickly went out to buy us a coffee pot, filters and coffee.

After my mom left, she sweetly left us the coffee pot for future visits. After a year in the tiny apartment, we upgraded to a bigger one. I brought the coffee pot and the filters along with us. We made coffee on rare occasions, and I was happy we were prepared.

When my husband and I finished schooling, we moved to another city for further training. As I packed the house for the move, I broke the coffee pot and decided to throw it away. However, I kept the coffee filters. There were a bunch of them, and I didn't want to waste a perfectly usable product. So I put the filters in a plastic bag and packed them.

My husband and I moved into our first home. We were excited about the change and the new possibilities that came with it. Most of all, we were thrilled that we lived right next to a local coffee shop. I didn't need to buy a coffee pot; and as the years went by, I completely forgot about the filters.

We moved one more time back to our hometown where my husband and I first met. As I was unpacking, I found the coffee filters. My husband must have tossed them into the box. I thought it was interesting that the filters had made it from our first home to our current home almost eight years later.

"What am I going to do with these filters?" I thought.

I kept them mainly for nostalgia's sake. The filters were a sweet reminder of my marriage's beginning. Finally, back in our hometown, we joined a church and began to raise our growing family. A year later we started a church homegroup. My friend bought me a coffee pot for Christmas, and I started serving the much-wanted coffee for my friends. I finally had a use for my coffee filters.

What I've come to understand is that God many times gives us coffee filters. He puts desires, talents, promises or dreams into our hearts way before we will ever use them. They just sit on the back burner, and we wonder why God ever gave us the passion in the first place.

But slowly, without us even realizing it, a need will arise and we'll finally get to do what God has called us to do. I don't know why God places these dreams in our hearts so early, but I do know that we will greatly enjoy dedicating ourselves to those dreams when the time arrives.... I was excited to finally use my filters.

"For no matter how many promises God has made, they are 'Yes' in Christ. And so through him the 'Amen' is spoken by us to the glory of God" (2 Corinthians 1.20 NIV).

Unpacking with God

My family and I recently moved back into our home on North Padre Island, the barrier island located near Corpus Christi, Texas, which I just learned is the longest barrier island in the world. Over two years ago after our move off "The Island" (as it's locally called) and into the city, I vowed never to move again.

Moving causes such stress and chaos and enormous amounts of work and patience.

But like God does, He moves us when He wants, regardless of our whimsical declarations. As I sit to write this at my desk in my new "old" home, memories of last week's process of methodically going through each room and every box, placing everything back where it belongs or finding new homes for them, is still fresh on my mind.

When I finally finished a few nights ago, I held up my hands and told my husband, "These hands have touch literally every single thing in this house."

As I thought about the last few weeks of craziness, God paralleled the order of my home to the order of my life. God is the maker of creativity (He created the solar system, angels, earth, animals and people), but He is also the maker of order. He has placed a system that arranges all of life, including salvation through His Son, Jesus. Without order even the most imaginative vision or idea would never come to fruition.

God wants to order our lives, not through control or coercion, but through the gentle leading of the Holy Spirit. God desires to place His hands on every detail of our lives because He loves us and He is working for our good. He doesn't want to cause us pain, but He knows that the abundant life that He has for us only comes with total submission to Him.

Sometimes we want to keep some boxes or rooms closed to God. We fear His rejection or His authority in our lives, but we must trust that He is the Master Organizer. He alone can make our lives peaceful and beautiful. If we open our hearts, minds and souls to Him, a mess may come forth; but we know that in due time, He will have arranged and organized even the darkest corners of our lives.

"He heals the brokenhearted and bandages their wounds. He counts the stars and calls them all by name. How great is our Lord! His power is absolute! His understanding is beyond comprehension!" (Psalm 147.3-5 NLT).

A Mess in His Hands

Have you ever seen the mess under your table after a full day of kid occupation and demolition? Gathering under your table are portions of pancake and bits of bacon from breakfast; glints of goldfish and hunks of ham from lunch; scattered salmon and messy mashed potatoes from dinner, and don't even get me started on the ever-accumulating pesky pieces of play dough, fragments of forgotten toys and determined debris from the yard.

You look at the mess under your table and become overwhelmed. "I just cleaned all this mess yesterday!" Then, your mind begins its spiral into a dismal recount of all the housekeeping you do every second of the day—cooking, organizing, cleaning messes, picking up toys, folding laundry and that's just the stuff you do at home!

I remember on one particular evening I finally cracked! I was so upset about the mess in the kitchen. It felt as though I looked away for one second and a tornado pointed its tricky finger down from the ceiling, stirring the contents of my kitchen into disarray. My mind started fuming, and I took a nose dive into my own pity party.

I angrily got the broom and started sweeping under the table. I filled my mind with all the little and seemingly insignificant things I do all day long. I questioned my purpose and the meaning of life, which at the time felt like it was all about cleaning. I had no peace or joy, and I forgot all of the blessings God pours on me each day.

About one minute later my floor was clean (all that complaining for something that was so easy to do)! I walked over to the trashcan to dump out that day's destruction, and I noticed how little the mess looked in the dustpan. I stared at the gathered garbage and laughed. I could hold all of it in the palm of my hand.

How could such a little mess cause me so much grief?

That's when God gave me an important image. I know it sounds cliché, but I imagined all of my life's problems in the palm of His hand, and they seemed small.

Everything is small compared to the power and love of God. If we give our lives over to Him, we are protected for eternity. Nothing can snatch us out of His hands. Though the messes of life—busyness, illness, divorce and death—surround us; we know that our Heavenly Father is holding them all in His mighty hand. He doesn't promise that our lives will be easy; He simple promises that we will be able to persevere (James 1.12).

"I give them eternal life, and they shall never perish; no one can snatch them out of my hand" (John 10.28 NIV).

Potty Training

I know that many women have been able to potty train their kids overnight, but that has never been the case for me. Whenever I read an article that boasts, "Potty train your toddler in 24 hours," I want to laugh.

All their lives, toddlers have been doing their business in a diaper, and overnight they are expected to change everything they are comfortable with and used to…?

Come on, now! How is that possible?

Yes, I know some people have experienced that potty-miracle, but not me; and I suspect many others haven't experienced that miracle either.

My second-born son is now almost three, and I must confess, I so wanted to keep a diaper on him until he turned 16. I have a lot of regrets from potty training my first-born, and I was not looking forward to rehearsing all my mistakes.

This time I was determined to have realistic goals for my son. I decided to be a big ball of spiritual fruits—patience, kindness, self-control, etc. It has been two months since I started potty training my son, and he will go pee-pee in the toilet; but he still will not go poo-poo (you can add your own euphemism).

When I first started potty training my second son, he wouldn't even sit on the toilet, let alone do his business. He was scared of it. So my only goal has been to de-fear him.

Everyday my son sits on the toilet after we eat lunch, and we play. I read him books, we sing songs, we play games…I do everything to make the toilet a fun place to be. I will continue to work towards making him feel comfortable, while demanding and expecting nothing from him.

Though he hasn't as yet completed the desired goal, I'm still proud of him. He has come a long way from the boy crying gator-tears, sitting with his legs in the air on the toilet. He now sits comfortably, while laughing and smiling.

Would you mind if I tied this potty experience into something that God taught me? He doesn't waste a good metaphor, does He?

God is constantly training us to be more Christ-like, and change is very hard. I have a friend who moved and lost all of her spiritual-support group. She is alone in another country, and she is having difficulty being intimate with God. She is very relational and not having the influences of her Christian friends has created a gap in her spiritual-growth—a gap that God wants to fill.

She says that she doesn't feel God doing anything with her. She doesn't feel any great movements of the Holy Spirit. She wonders if she is doing something wrong.

I told her, "You are doing something right!"

God is allowing my friend to get comfortable just being with Him without her usual infrastructure of spiritual help. He is not pushing her or expecting much of her; He just wants her to get used to this new level of intimacy. Once she is comfortable, He'll be ready to ask more of her.

"For my yoke is easy and my burden is light" (Matthew 11.30 NIV).

Glory Inside

I enjoy giving my kids massages about once a week. I know that the movement and light pressure on their skin and muscles help with the cardiovascular and lymphatic systems, thereby improving overall health. Plus, it's an excuse for me to love on them in a tangible way. My kids have gotten so used to their weekly rubdowns that they run to the massage table with smiles and eagerly stretch out ready to relax.

One particular afternoon, the weather was very stormy. You could hear the rain beating down on the roof and the thunder rolling and lightning cracking outside. It was a great excuse for a massage, since we couldn't go anywhere or play outside.
I usually massage my daughter first. She's the youngest and her little frame makes her easy to massage. Then, I massage my middle boy. Finally, I massage my oldest son who is nine years old. He loves his massages and talks the entire time, knowing he has my full attention.

I listen to a Christian singer, Michelle Tumes, while I massage. I love the soft sound of her music and the promise-filled lyrics of her songs. I had to turn up the volume because the thunder and lightning roared outside. Inside my heart, I thought about how much beauty was in the moment–the roaring thunder mixed with the glorious music. My son must have shared my feelings.

He said, "Isn't it amazing how it is thundering outside, but we are safe inside. It's like God's glory. Sometimes the world is dark and scary, but in God we are safe and surrounded by His love."

Wow! What a precious thought from the lips of a nine-year-old. Yes, the world can be dark and scary, but in God we have nothing to fear. God loves us and sent His Son, Jesus, to die on the cross, so we could have an eternal relationship with Him. If the God of the Universe is with us in the middle of the storm, what do we have to fear?

 "The LORD is with me; I will not be afraid. What can mere mortals do to me?" (Psalm 118.6 NIV).

Talking with God

I allow each of my boys to pray at night as they are lying in bed. My youngest boy is three and my oldest is five. The youngest one usually prays and his older brother then follows.

At first my youngest boy didn't want to pray because he was embarrassed. He didn't pray like his older brother, and I think that made him self-conscious. However, I encouraged him without any pressured expectations, and he started to pray now and then.

One night, my youngest son jumped into praying. He prayed for juice, toys, cookies, popcorn, etc. I could hear my oldest son snickering under his breath. When my youngest son said, "Amen," I kissed him and went over to my oldest son's bed.

I whispered in his ear, "You used to pray like that. He will get better and better as he practices. Let's not make fun of him, okay?"

My oldest son looked grave and nodded his head in agreement. He then prayed his prayer with confidence. He asked God to bless our family and protect us while we slept. I kissed him goodnight, turned off the lights and shut the door behind me.

Prayer is often so misunderstood. There are people who can pray all the pretty religious phrases and others who are straightforward. They are all beautiful as long as the motive is right. What is the motive of prayer? To speak to God.

We have an amazing line of communication to God, and it takes time to get the hang of it. We must not beat ourselves up if we feel like we didn't pray right. God hears the heart, not the words. The only way to get better at talking with God is to practice—practice makes perfect!

Do you feel like your prayers are hitting the ceiling? Be honest with God, and He will meet you where you are at. He wants to communicate with you more than anything.

And just remember that when there are no more words, the Holy Spirit prays on your behalf!

"I pray for them. I am not praying for the world, but for those you have given me, for they are yours" (John 17.9 NIV).

Boats and Promises

My family and I went to what we call "Angel Island," which is a small patch of dirt in the middle of a canal in the Laguna Madre. We like this little island because the kids can't wander off, and we can watch the boats and the skiers as they jet on by. On the other side of the canal on this particular day were two dogs. Their owners landed their boat on the strip of land adjacent to us, and the dogs enjoyed running up and down the length of the shore.

Whenever a boat or jet skier would drive by, one of the dogs would chase it until he ran out of land. He would start at one end of the strip and run the distance of a football field to the other end. The boats were going about 35 mph, and this dog kept pace! I couldn't believe how fast he ran and how excited he looked chasing these boats.

I felt kind of bad for the dog, though. He never caught the boats. The land would run out and the boats would zip on passed him. The dog didn't seem to mind because he would go back to where he started and wait for another boat to come. I think the dog loved the thrill of chasing the boats. He didn't really need to catch them.

This made me think of God's promises to us. I've realized that God always puts His promises to us way out in the distance. They are almost never within our immediate reach. In order to claim these promises, we have to get our running shoes on and chase them.

"Why do you make it so hard, God?" I asked Him.

God whispered into my heart: "Those promises mean very little to me, but you mean everything to me. I place those promises away from you so you can move from Point A (old selfish nature) to Point B (Christ-likeness). I want you close to me, so I place promises along the way to draw you near and to teach, encourage and bless you."

Finally, after years of waiting on God to fulfill His promises to me, I understood what I was doing wrong. God's promises are already fulfilled. If He gave them to me, they are recorded in history as completed and I shouldn't worry about the timing. What I need to focus on is the chase. How am I running after my promises? Am I focused like that dog with his huge grin and tongue lolling out to one side? Or am I whining and complaining to God that He is taking too long and He is making it too hard?

I think God wants us to enjoy the chase. He put promises around us to make life fun and rewarding. He didn't put them there to make us miserable. My goal for myself now is to enjoy the chase. Chasing dreams is a privilege, and God has given me gifts, talents and the Holy Spirit to help me run to win.

Unlike the dog, if I run out of land, God will teach me to run on water, so I can continue to chase my boat. And when I finally catch it, I want to be eager for another promise and another chase! Promises help me to cultivate a deeper relationship with God, so I want to chase after a bunch of them! I desire for Jesus to be my best friend before I meet Him face to face.

"I have sought your face with all my heart; be gracious to me according to your promise" (Psalm 119.58 NIV).

Eternally New

I downloaded a song that has really spoken to my heart. My nine-year-old son loves the song too. We listen to it together, and we discuss the spiritual themes.

One morning while cooking breakfast, I had the song on repeat on my phone. My kids patiently sat in their chairs at the breakfast table, as I scrambled up some eggs and ham for them. I could tell that they enjoyed the song, since they were each waiting quietly for breakfast.

The song finally ended after about five repeats, and my son suddenly said, "Turn off the song, Mom! I don't want to listen to it again."

I know my son. I'm aware that the song is still fresh and beautiful to him. So I had a sneaking suspicion about why he wanted me to turn off the music. I pushed the stop button on my phone and asked, "Why don't you want to listen to the song anymore?"

My theory was correct. He said, "Because I don't want to get tired of the song. I like it, but if you play it too much, I will get used to it."

Thus the temptation people face in life: we struggle not to take things for granted. We get accustomed to people, places, situations and things; and we lose the luster of our original feelings of awe and adoration.

It takes work to keep the emotional "wow factor" alive. But I think humility plays a big part in maintaining our childlike wonderment. Once we admit that our understanding is not the end-all, we can eagerly look forward to experiencing, learning and discovering more.

This is especially true for our relationship with Jesus. We can't allow our relationship with Him to stagnate. The more we grow in our intimacy with our Savior, the more we realize that He is so wonderfully beyond our full comprehension. How could we ever take an all-encompassing God for granted?

When we seek Him everyday, we begin to recognize that there is so much more to understand about His character, His love and His Kingdom. Knowing God is a never-ending journey that we all can look forward to.

"But those who wish to boast should boast in this alone: that they truly know me and understand that I am the Lord who demonstrates unfailing love and who brings justice and righteousness to the earth, and that I delight in these things. I, the Lord, have spoken!" (Jeremiah 9.24 NLT).

Music Flaws in Glory

My sons both take piano lessons, and a few times a year, they have a recital. Their spring recital this year was held at a local church, and a gorgeous ebony piano patiently waited for all the children as they took their turns.

The longer musical pieces were saved for the end, and I knew one particular boy would be doing his last. He's about sixteen years old, and he always chooses unique, complicated songs to play.

This year, he decided to play a song that I knew well. I read the title of the song and the name of the Christian band on the very last line of the recital program. I enjoyed each performance, especially my two sons' moments on center stage (they did an amazing job!), but I couldn't wait to hear one of my favorite Christian songs played live on the piano.

When the young man began to play, I recognized the tune instantly. A flood of emotions for our Lord filled me. I could hear the lyrics of God's truth and beauty run through my mind. Even though I tried to hold back the tears, many of them slipped down my cheeks.

As the song progressed, the young man struggled with the complicated formation of piano notes. He had to pause several times, and his expression became tense and a little frustrated. I prayed for him to continue with the song because all I heard was the glorious love of God. His mistakes could not take away from special feelings welling up in my heart.

And I know that God feels the same way about us. When we commit to creating beauty for God on this earth in obedience to the Holy Spirit, we will always make mistakes. But God's love overpowers our flawed efforts, and all of creation only senses the sound of His glory through our lives.

Sometimes I focus so much on my mistakes that I forget that God's grace creates beauty from the ashes. I will not let fear stop me from playing my life's song for the Lord. I will not let my weaknesses prevent me from doing my best for my Savior. I want to be like that young man playing the piano: he made mistakes but he finished his performance to the end. All to the glory of God!

"To all who mourn in Israel, he will give a crown of beauty for ashes, a joyous blessing instead of mourning, festive praise instead of despair. In their righteousness, they will be like great oaks that the Lord has planted for his own glory" (Isaiah 61.3 NLT).

A Tooth Moral

I gave my eldest son (nine years old) one of my old cameras. He loves to use it to take photos of his beloved plants. One night, my middle child (seven years old) was just about to lose his second tooth. This tooth had been loose for over a week, and I knew it was hanging by a thread—or better yet a root!

So I thought I would have a little fun with this tooth. I asked my seven-year-old, Levi, if he wanted me to take out this tooth like grandma used to take out mine. He said yes. So I told him that I would be tying one end of the floss around his tooth and the other end around the bathroom door handle. He was so excited!

My oldest son, Isaac, started recording the process. When I was done tying the floss, I took over filming and asked Isaac to help his brother shut the door. He argued that he wanted to record. I again asked him to help his brother. He argued again. The third time I patiently repeated my request, and after another round of arguments, he finally obeyed.

I then proceeded to record the funniest home video tooth extraction that I've ever seen. My boys peeled with laughter, along with the rest of the family. I put the video on Facebook, and it became an instant hit! Isaac and Levi just shined with boyish fun.

Later on that evening, I showed the video to Isaac, my oldest, and explained an important lesson to him.

"Do you see how much you shined in the video," I said.

"Yes, Levi and I had so much fun," he agreed.

"Would you be in the video if I didn't film for you and ask you to help Levi?" I asked.

He thought for a moment, knowing I was just about to expose the moral of the story.

"No," he finally answered.

"You resisted being obedient three times," I began. "And you almost missed out on being a part of this fun experience with Levi. All I wanted to do was let you shine. That is why I wanted to hold the camera."

"I'm sorry, Mom," he said.

"It's okay," I answered, giving him a big hug. "I just want you to remember that God will ask you to do things that go against what you want to do. But you need to realize that God wants you to shine too. He will only ask you to do things that shine His glory in your life. You might not understand God's will at first, but you can trust that He will accomplish great things in your life if you stay obedient to Him."

"He replied, 'Blessed rather are those who hear the word of God and obey it'" (Luke 11.28 NIV).

Swollen Ankles and Pedicures

When I was almost eight months pregnant with my third child, my feet and legs swelled with edema. The areas between my ankles and calf muscles were especially waterlogged. I tried to rub my legs, but my protruding belly made bending over very difficult.

Finally, I decided to treat myself to a pedicure. I wanted my toes to look manicured and painted for my impending date with the hospital bed. Plus, I knew that many nail technicians offer a small leg massage as part of the pedicure service, so I hoped to get a little relief from the pressure in my legs.

When I arrived at the nail salon, the lady giving me a pedicure was a few months pregnant with her second child. We shared baby and pregnancy stories, and she proceeded to massage my legs—especially the areas most swollen—for a full twenty minutes each! All I could do was lie back and tell her how good the rub down felt.

My tender, swollen muscles relaxed under the firm and consistent pressure of her hands. It was like she knew exactly the discomfort I was going through and precisely how she could alleviate some of the pain. I couldn't help giving her a large tip because she had read my mind and gave me the one thing I most desperately wanted at the moment: a leg massage!

As I drove home feeling so blessed that this woman went out of her way to serve me, I realized something valuable. The woman knew where I hurt the most because she had probably suffered from edema herself. She understood my discomfort, so she was better able to provide me much needed relief!

God allows us to go through difficult times, and He doesn't waste any of our pain. Not only does our suffering help us to become more like Christ, it also becomes a tool for us to serve others who face similar trials. We can offer support to people who are struggling in circumstances that we have already overcome.

Most importantly, though, we can know that we always have the ultimate victory in Christ because Jesus has already overcome the world!

 "I have told you all this so that you may have peace in me. Here on earth you will have many trials and sorrows. But take heart, because I have overcome the world" (John 16.33 NLT).

The Fog of Love

My mother came to visit us for my older sister's 40th birthday. My mom, my twin and I all threw my sister a Fabulous and Forty hot pink and zebra birthday party. We had games, a candy bar and lots of Mexican food! It was a blast, and my older sister was so blessed! She'll have memories to keep for a lifetime.

The following Monday, I got up early to take my mom to the airport. We live in a beach town, so sometimes the winter gulf breeze cools the water vapors inland to their dew point, and fog forms over the coastal area. It was early in the morning, and the sun hadn't risen to disperse the thick fog. I had to drive my mother through layers of white fog, barely able to see the street signs in front of me.

I felt tense the entire drive, and I even missed the airport exit and had to get off the highway and turn around. I normally don't mind the fog, but I felt pressure to get my mother to the airport safely and on time. I was so relieved when we made it! My mother and I prayed, and I watched her walk to the terminal.

On the way home, the fog was still thick, but the tension I felt earlier abated. I realized how much stress I was carrying because I love my mom and I care for her safety. Love is an extremely heavy burden when we forgot that God is ultimately in charge. God loves my mother more than I do; and no matter what happens, He is carrying her life in His hands.

I want to love others and serve in the capacity to which I'm called, but I also need to admit that I can't carry the burden of love alone. I am not perfect, and I can't cause the sun to rise and vanquish the fog. But there is a God in heaven Who is mighty and powerful. He loves us with an unfailing love and His purposes are always for our good. I can rely on God to give me strength when I need it, and I can trust that not even the fog surprises Him.

"Fear not, for I am with you; be not dismayed, for I am your God; I will strengthen you, I will help you, I will uphold you with my righteous right hand" (Isaiah 41.10 ESV).

Hand of Pretense

"Let each of you look not only to his own interests, but also to the interests of others" (Philippians 2.4 ESV).

My husband and I brought our kids to a large, local park sprawled along the gulf rim of our coastal town on an unseasonably warm winter's day. It seemed that our entire city had the same notion; and skateboarders, children and picnickers savored the sunlit landscape, playing and lounging upon the wide-lipped grassy valley. That day was a pleasant reprieve from our busy, cold holiday schedule; and I immersed myself in the special moment with my family.

We had come to this park many times, and my boys always watched with wonderment as the big kids skated and biked the dips and curves of the cement skate park. Now, it was their turn to enjoy the concrete waves with their own bikes and feel the thrill of sliding down the smooth slopes. My husband stood as an audience of one in a crowd of many, clapping and cheering two boys that emulated his laughter and resembled his smile.

I rolled my four-year-old daughter's bike to the long curvy sidewalk that skirted the shoreline. When we got to a safe point on the trail, I helped her climb unto the pink seat and placed her feet securely on the pedals. I have to admit that she looked so sweet sitting on her pink and purple bicycle that was fitted with training wheels and sparkly streamers. Her little princess helmet held safely to her head, and she gave me a determined, "Let's go, Mommy!"

My daughter can ride her bike fairly well, since the training wheels keep her balanced, but she likes the feel of my hand on her back. My hand gives her a sense of security and lets her know that I am near. I took in the scenery as I casually followed my daughter down the winding path. I must have become distracted by all the movement around me because my daughter's bike hit a rocky patch, and she fell onto the grass lining the sidewalk.

She wasn't hurt, but she was upset that I had let her fall. It took her a while to trust that my hand would catch her if she lost her balance again. I realized that I had allowed my hand to become a facade of safety. In actuality, I wasn't paying attention to my little girl riding her bike. I was lost in my own world of thoughts.

And I wonder how many times we miss the pain of those around us because we are so distracted. We are distracted by our own worries, by social media, by our busy schedules, by our ambitions and by our choices. We are lost in a world of me-centered living, and our hand of support is one of mere pretense. The truth is that our hands can't reach the lives of everyone, but they can touch the souls that God has placed nearest to us.

I think the best antidote to our me-centered distractions is to be God-centered. God loves His children, and He longs to work through us to support those around us. When we focus on God, He will place the ones we can serve within arm's reach. When we align our hearts with His, we will eventually gain a love that cannot be shaken or moved by daily distractions. Then we will be better aware when someone enters a rocky patch and quicker to offer our hand of support when they fall.

"God is not unjust; he will not forget your work and the love you have shown him as you have helped his people and continue to help them" (Hebrews 6.10 NIV).

The Gift of Giving

Isaac, my nine-year-old son, walked up to me and sighed. "I'm never going to get a dinosaur," he lamented. He sat down at the table and put his head in his hands.

We were at a pizza and game restaurant for kids, and my son had used up all of his coins on a claw machine filled with dinosaurs. Try as he may, Isaac wasn't able to take hold of a dinosaur long enough so it could fall down the winning shoot.

"I'm sorry," I said, knowing my son's intense personality. I've come to realize that accepting disappointment will always be a struggle for him. He had sacrificed all of his coins only to come back empty-handed.

Suddenly, my six-year-old son, Levi, came running up. "I won it! I won it!" he yelled and handed a green dinosaur to his older brother.

Instantly, Isaac's face lit up. "Thank you, Levi!" he cried and grabbed hold of the dinosaur, holding it to his chest. I stared at my boys, excited that the problem had been solved so quickly and without my assistance.

Both my sons smiled happily, and I could tell that Levi found immense pleasure in blessing his brother. Finally, Isaac suggested Levi try to win another dinosaur for himself and one for their sister.

When my sons returned to me five minutes later, Levi had won eight dinosaurs. I couldn't believe it! God had blessed Levi with a bevy of different dinosaurs, which he shared with his sister and brother. Plus, God had handed me an excellent, ready-to-be-used teachable moment!

"You see what happens when we give something special to others? God is able to bless us with so much more! Levi, you gave your only dinosaur to Isaac because you love him, and God blessed you with eight more! When we bless others, God will bless us."

My kids all nodded, and I was excited that I could teach them a difficult truth from a reality that they could understand. "Thank you, Lord!"

"Give, and you will receive. Your gift will return to you in full—pressed down, shaken together to make room for more, running over, and poured into your lap. The amount you give will determine the amount you get back" (Luke 6.38 NLT).

Stumbling Gracefully

I used to struggle with self-condemnation. Many times on my race of faith, I would stumble. Even though my heart is for God, my sin nature gets in the way and causes my feet to trip. However, instead of getting up, dusting myself off and continuing my run, I would sit where I had fallen and sulk.

I'd fret over my stupid mistake. I would drive the screwdriver of shame just a little deeper. I would self-analyze every inch of my fall on instant replay, watching it over and over again. All the while the race moved on, and I remained sitting in the middle of the track in self-defeat.

The Holy Spirit has exposed the selfish default setting of my human nature. I know that sin will always be a part of my life; though, hopefully, its grip will loosen as I become more like Jesus. So the fact that I will stumble should not be a surprise anymore.

I finally realized the problem isn't that I stumble; the problem is that I get stuck in the stumble.

God has shown me something beautiful that has given me the ability to stumble gracefully. One afternoon, my family and I were walking through a plant nursery. It had rained earlier that morning, so there were many dips in the ground filled with muddy water. I walked with my daughter and pointed out all the mud-laden holes, so she could avoid stepping in them.

The Holy Spirit whispered to me, "That's why I convict you of sin. I'm not condemning you. I'm pointing out the potholes, so you can avoid stepping in them."

Jesus came to this world not to condemn us, but to save us from the traps of the Enemy. Conviction should not carry a sting, because Jesus took that sting upon Himself on the cross. We no longer have to bear the weight of condemnation, because we have been made righteous through Jesus Christ.

The courts of heaven declare us forgiven of all wrong. Jesus sealed the covenant of our righteousness with His blood. So when the Holy Spirit convicts us, we should not feel shame. Instead, we should feel the love of Jesus overflowing from the cross. Jesus was broken by sin, so we could be healed by grace.

So when the Holy Spirit points out a sin in my life, I no longer allow guilt to claim dominance over me. I push passed my pride and enjoy the peace that humility and thanksgiving provide. I reach for Christ's love, pick myself up, dust myself off and run my race in the freedom of grace!

"God made him who had no sin to be sin for us, so that in him we might become the righteousness of God" (2 Corinthians 5.21 NIV).

A Self-Portrait of Faith

My four-year-old daughter loves to draw self-portraits. She makes a big circle in the middle of the page, which represents her body. Then, she attaches four lines to the circle, which signify her arms and legs. She puts small circles at the end of each line to form her hands and feet. Finally, she creates a tuft of scribbles on top of the circle to show that she, indeed, has hair. On special occasions, she'll draw a big bow next to her self-portrait to represent the enormous collection of bows she has acquired.

Her portraits are very rudimentary and simplistic, but they do capture the basic elements of her person—body, limbs, hair, etc. Oh! And I forgot to mention that she always places a big smiley face on the egg-shaped body. She by all accounts is a happy and contented little girl!

When we first accept Jesus into our hearts and form a relationship with Him, our understanding of Him will be much like my daughter's self-portrait. We won't comprehend all the finer details of faith, but we will know for certain that we have been saved. As we grow in the Lord, our portraits of faith will become more sophisticated and detailed; however, the basic elements of faith will always remain: Jesus gave us His holiness, so we can have a right-standing with God even in our sinful state.

The problem arises when we try to explain the detailed depiction of Christ to non-Christians when they still can't comprehend the most basic of design. How can unbelievers envision the shading of a cheekbone when they can't see the face? Having theological debates with people who don't know God is like witnessing in a foreign language. Nothing will make sense unless the spiritual language of belief is opened to them.

So before we make a stand about finer facets of our faith, we might want to make sure that our audience has grasped the foundation of faith: Jesus! Once they accept Jesus as their Lord and Savior, the Holy Spirit can then use our words to lead them into a more intimate and vibrant relationship with Christ.

"He is the radiance of the glory of God and the exact imprint of his nature, and he upholds the universe by the word of his power. After making purification for sins, he sat down at the right hand of the Majesty on high" (Hebrews 1.3 ESV).

The Weight of Unrest

I have given birth to three amazing children, and after each pregnancy, I had a lot of pounds to shed. I gained 55lbs with my first child, 45lbs with my second child and 35lbs with my third child; and for an entire year after the delivery day, I struggled to fit back into my clothes. I had very little to wear because my pre-pregnancy clothes were too small and my maternity clothes were too big, and I wouldn't allow myself to buy new clothes.

After my first two babies were born, I lived with great unrest and lost my peace because I became too self-focused and overly worried about losing weight. I was filled with guilt if I didn't work out or if I ate something high in calories. However, by the third baby, I knew the routine, and I was better able to trust that "this too shall pass." Losing weight is a difficult task, but I wasn't going to forsake my joy over a slice of pizza or a missed day at the gym.

Any struggle that we allow to take our focus off of the Lord and onto ourselves and our circumstances, will cause unrest in our lives. When we lose sight of Jesus, we will begin to lose our peace and joy, and our struggle will wreak havoc in our minds and hearts. Although it took me a few years, I have learned to trust my strength in the Lord and not allow my focus to stay centered on my struggle. We can have peace in our difficulty when we focus on God and His great love for us.

"For the Lord your God is living among you. He is a mighty savior. He will take delight in you with gladness. With his love, he will calm all your fears. He will rejoice over you with joyful songs" (Zephaniah 3.17 NLT).

Looking Back

My kids love to show me stuff. Whether it is a picture they drew, a room they cleaned or a Lego construction they created—they want to ensure that their mommy gives them the proper accolades and attention for their work. Every day at least one of my kids runs up to me, yelling, "Mommy! Mommy! Come look at what I did!"

They also come get me when they need help or when something is wrong. They may need help finding their shoes or someone may have gotten hurt or something accidentally broke. They want me to take care of the problem, so they rush to me in desperate pursuit, crying, "Mommy! Come quick! We need you!"

They pull my hand to follow them and rush in front of me, so they can lead the way. I follow behind them and watch the direction of their steps, preparing myself for the surprise that awaits us.

I've noticed that as they walk, they are constantly looking over their shoulders, making sure that I'm still behind them. Once they locate me with their eyes, they forge forward on their quest.

Isn't it nice to know that we never have to look behind us when we walk by faith?

The Bible says that God goes before us, preparing our way (Exodus 23.20).

He will never leave us stranded or alone (Hebrews 13.5).

We don't have to constantly look over our shoulder, looking for God, because He sees our hard work and knows our pain. God is not surprised by our circumstances, and He already has His favor and grace ready for us.

"The Lord himself goes before you and will be with you; he will never leave you nor forsake you. Do not be afraid; do not be discouraged" (Deuteronomy 31.8 NIV).

The Winners

The Encouragement

"Therefore encourage one another and build one another up, just as you are doing" (1 Thessalonians 5.11 ESV).

My husband ran Beach to Bay, which is a relay marathon in our hometown of Corpus Christi, TX. He ran the fourth leg of the race out of six; but toward the end of his almost 5-mile run, he began to lose steam. Though he knew it had to be close, he began to walk the last half mile of the race. He was exhausted.

A woman jogging a medium cadence came up behind him. She wasn't about to let my 6'5" athletically built husband ease his way to the finish line. She started yelling "encouragement" at him.

"Pick up the pace!" she called. "Don't you dare walk. Get moving! You're going to run to the end."

My husband shrugged his shoulders and began to jog once more. A few seconds later he saw the finish line, and he began to run faster. Once he saw his relay partner, he was in an all-out sprint before he passed the baton.

The Jealousy

My three-year daughter fell into a pool near the steps where my five-year-old son was standing. As my husband ran to retrieve her, our son grabbed her out of the water and held her. We were all so excited because our son saved his little sister. However, our seven-year-old son who was next to his father at the time became angry.

When I asked him what was wrong, he said, "I wanted to save her!"

I explained to him that he should be happy for his brother's victory. I said that I was proud of both my boys, and I reminded my eldest of all of his many victories. I could tell he understood, but it was still hard for him to encourage his brother.

I realized that there are situations in our lives where it is easy to encourage others, but there are other situations where it is more difficult. And I wondered what made the difference.

The Difference

The woman who encouraged my husband was not in the race to win. She probably ran for enjoyment or for a feeling of accomplishment, but she was not one of the professionals who fly from distant lands to our little city to compete for a prize. Some of the teams running in our marathon invest great amounts of money, sweat and time to win. And I can almost guarantee that they are not encouraging their competitors to pick up the pace! Although her encouragement is greatly valued and shows her care for others, it comes from someone who has nothing to lose or prove—she wasn't interested in first prize. She was having a good time and enjoyed gathering others in her bubble of joy.

On the other hand, my eldest son invests a great deal into his relationship with his sister. He holds her in the pool when they swim together, he compliments her wardrobe, he prays with her and—like his younger brother—he loves her. So when his brother won "first prize"—which is probably how he viewed it—he became jealous. He wanted to win, so it was hard for him to encourage his brother. He had to make the choice to do it anyway.

The Reasons

I believe there are two reasons that prevent us from encouraging one another. The first reason is that we have not asked God what He has planned for our lives. If we knew the victories God has already won for us, we would not covet the victories of others. I can be happy for missionaries in foreign countries because I know that I'm not called to it. I can be happy for worship leaders because I know that I'm not called to it. I am a writer. It may not be glamorous. I may type in my pajamas. I may not be around a lot of people. But I'm called to it!

However, it used to be hard for me to encourage other writers—especially writers similar to me—who are publishing, who are making a difference for Christ, who are so extremely gifted that they seem to create syntactical symphonies everywhere they go. I had to choose to encourage them. I used to examine all of the effort, time and resources I invested into sharpening my craft, and I'd wonder, "Why can't I win first place?" But after watching my son's difficulty with encouraging his brother, I understood the second reason it is difficult to encourage others: We forget that God's favor, His blessings, and His victories are not finite—they are infinite, boundless and limitless!

The Prize

God has all the natural and supernatural resources at His disposal, and He can choose to make more whenever He pleases. He wants to bless His children, and He has an infinite amount of victories available for each of us. We don't have to be jealous of the people winning to our right and to our left because He has a path of wins right in front of us. When we choose to encourage those around us, we show God that we believe in His unlimited favor, we believe that He has great things planned for us, we believe that His glory has an endless supply, and we believe that He desires all of us to win!

So instead of being jealous, let us believe that we will all be standing across the finish line of heaven—each wearing our individually tailored victor's crown and gold medal. We can joyfully encourage others in this race of life because our Father has a first prize for each of us that only we can claim. God has already won it for us; we just need to reach out and grab it!

"Don't you realize that in a race everyone runs, but only one person gets the prize? So run to win! All athletes are disciplined in their training. They do it to win a prize that will fade away, but we do it for an eternal prize. So I run with purpose in every step. I am not just shadowboxing" (1 Corinthians 9.24-26 NLT).

Multiple Choice

I enjoy homeschooling my kids. I get to watch their learning progress and help them along the way. One skill to which I pay particular attention is discerning the correct answer for multiple-choice. I know that many of the standardized tests that they will take in life will have multiple choice questions, so I want to ensure that my kids have mastered the discipline. If they don't know the process of answering multiple-choice questions, the test grades will not be able to accurately display their knowledge.

I noticed that one of my sons makes a fundamental mistake when answering multiple-choice questions that most young students make: He answers the multiple-choice without reading all of the possible answers. When he reads an answer that seems to fit, he forgoes reading the rest of the list. This habit may cause him to miss the question even if he truly knows the answer.

When I see my son make this hasty mistake, I stop him and have him read the entire list aloud. Many times he keeps his original answer, but there are other times that he switches his answer to the correct one further down the list. I have to explain to him that the answer he chose only sounds correct because he didn't read the rest of the list.

The same is true for Christians. God's understanding is beyond ours, and many times He moves in directions that we have never experienced before (Isaiah 55.9). Our limited point of view leaves room for only 1 or 2 possible answers, but with God all things are possible. God is creative, and He shows His amazing imagination in the world He has designed. There is no limit to what God can do; so before we circumvent His plan with our tiny sliver of understanding, we need to be patient and allow God to present His perfect answer.

"Jesus looked at them intently and said, 'Humanly speaking, it is impossible. But with God everything is possible'" (Matthew 19.26 NLT).

Wall Doorknob

The kids' area at our church is decorated like a beach boardwalk. There's a pretend movie theater, surf shop, ice cream parlor and candy store that make up the beachfront veneer. My daughter is particularly fascinated with the door that leads into the candy store. The tiny painted entrance is perfectly located between two store windows filled with an assortment of candy.

My daughter runs to the door and grabs hold of the shiny, silver doorknob; and she pulls and tugs, desperate to open it. She pleads with me to help pry the door open, but I know there is nothing to be done. The doorknob is actually bolted to a cement wall, and the doorframe surrounding it is simply a painted facade. The door is fake, the windows are fake, the store is fake and the entire boardwalk is fake.

I've tried to explain to her that the store is make-believe, but my words contradict the reality she thinks she sees with her eyes. As I watch my daughter struggle with believing me and trusting my words, I think about God's command to live by faith and not by sight (2 Corinthians 5.7).

Many times God allows the circumstances in our lives to "appear" as if they contradict with the promises He has for us. We hear the

Holy Spirit whisper one thing, but our eyes behold something quite different. Finally, we find ourselves at a crossroads: Who will we believe? God or our circumstances?

When our world seems to challenge God's whispers, we need to press into His Word, pursue Him in prayer and wait patiently for His will. God can be trusted, and He can do the impossible through us (Luke 1.37).

"Praise the Lord who has given rest to his people Israel, just as he promised. Not one word has failed of all the wonderful promises he gave through his servant Moses" (1 Kings 8.56 NLT).

Strike Three Epiphany

I went through a season when I didn't feel like I was doing much for God. I carried guilt and anxiety that I should be doing more. I don't know if I compared myself to my friends or if I desperately wanted the affirmation that "good works" afford, but somehow I found myself with an unhealthy opinion that I wasn't good enough.

At this time, I also had a baby, a two-year-old and a four-year-old. Looking back now, I should have known that I was doing an amazing work of God—raising future Kingdom Leaders—but the role of a mother plays out much like an unseen missionary. Sometimes you don't realize the pivotal part you play until you see the fruit forming in your children's lives. And very few people around you see the sacrifices you make and how hard you work.

Finally, one day I decided that I was going to do some street witnessing, carrying all my kids with me. I planned on buying Bibles and talking to three people each day about Jesus. I honestly must have been wearing rose-colored glasses because how anyone can get anything done with three needy bodies and souls with them 24/7 is beyond me.

The first day, I loaded the kids up in the car and drove to my first stop: Starbucks. I was going to talk to the drive-through barista about Jesus; and long lines, rushed orders and honking cars would not stop me! When I pulled up to the window, I instantly looked for something to say that would break the ice. When my barista took my tip, I noticed that he had a tattoo bandage covering his arm, so I asked him about his tattoo. He promptly exposed his ink and showed me an awesome illustration of the Holy Trinity across his forearm. He was a Christian.

Okay, I thought. I'll try again. So the kids and I headed to the carwash. I spotted a man brushing the sides of the cars with a large scrubber before they entered the hands-free car wash, and I prepared myself to talk to him about Jesus. After he finished scrubbing my car; I got my tip ready, handed it to him and just before I could form my first words, the man bowed his head and prayed right in front of me. He thanked God for the money, blessed it and anointed it for God's service. He was a Christian.

As I drove home, I looked for one more opportunity to share Christ. I had two strikes against me, but I would not give up the fight. Just before I got back on the highway, I saw a fireman holding a boot and standing on the corner of the street. He was collecting money for charity, so I grabbed the last bill in my wallet and rolled down my window. I handed him the money and began my intro into faith, but he interrupted me by saying my name. I looked at the fireman with surprise and took a better look at his face. I quickly realized that he and his wife attended my church and were members of my church homegroup. He was a Christian.

Once I got back onto the highway, I had to laugh. I asked God why He had creatively and sweetly sabotaged my street-witnessing venture. He simply said, "Because I haven't called you to it."

I realized several things from this experience. 1) Sometimes a good thing is not God's thing. 2) You should never do anything motivated by guilt. 3) God doesn't give you more than you can handle. 4) Raising kids is ministry. 5) Don't compare yourself to others. 6) Unseen ministries are no less important. 7) God sees and blesses everything done in secret.

Although I still struggle with feeling unimportant and passed-over, I know that I'm right where God wants me to be. When I focus on how much pleasure God gains from my obedience, I'm overwhelmed by His love and peace. I trust that God has great plans for me, and I don't need anyone to affirm my purpose because God's Word and Promise validate my life.

"For I know the plans I have for you," declares the Lord, "plans to prosper you and not to harm you, plans to give you hope and a future" (Jeremiah 29.11 NIV).

Only the Go-between

My friend does the coolest God-thing with her kids—she opens doors for God to show Himself to them. I've seen this happen several times in my experience, but I'm sure it's a consistent pattern in my friend's family.

One morning I was shopping and I felt the urge to buy my friend's daughter a pair of earrings. I brought the earrings to her little girl that afternoon; and after I presented them to her, my friend squatted down and told her, "You see! I told you God would bless you today!"

My friend's daughter was learning a new level of responsibility, and my friend encouraged her by telling her, "God is going to bless you for it!" Instead of blessing her daughter herself (which she easily could have done), she opened a door for God to show Himself—and He did!

I think many times that I, as a parent, get in the way of God blessing my children. I want so much to give them everything, but I need to leave room for God to show Himself. Everything comes from God, but my kids will have trouble understanding that unless I keep pointing the blessings back to Him.

They need to understand that I am merely a go-between. I am not the source of blessings. I want my kids to know that all good things come from God; so that when things happen that are out of my control, they know to look to Him.

"Praise be to the God and Father of our Lord Jesus Christ, who has blessed us in the heavenly realms with every spiritual blessing in Christ" (Ephesians 1.3 NIV).

Stuck

About six months ago my son moved from his highchair to a booster seat. We would buckle him into the seat and scoot him up to the table to eat. He started wanting to buckle himself into the booster seat, which was difficult because he had trouble clicking the latches together.

When he finally learned how to do it, he was ecstatic! Every time we would try to buckle him in, he would throw a fit. He wanted to do it all by himself. He continued to buckle himself every time he sat at the table, even when it was apparent that he no longer needed the support. My son didn't care. He liked the comfort and the routine of it.

However, there was one problem: He did not know how to unbuckle himself. My son is a slow eater, so sometimes I would leave him at the table so I could wash the dishes or change his baby brother's diaper. Many times I would hear him yelling, "Mommy, I'm done! Help me, Mommy! I'm done eating!" He wanted to get up and do something else; but because of his routine of buckling into the booster, he was stuck.

This example reminds me so much of us as Christians. We cling onto a routine or tradition so tightly that when God moves us in another direction, we're stuck. We don't know how to unbuckle ourselves from what we are comfortable with.

I wonder how many times we miss out on God's awesome plan because we continually go back to what is comfortable. If we strap ourselves into the same routines, we may miss out on the new movement of God. Feeling comfortable, secure and protected is wonderful; but if God is moving us, we need to let go of our traditions and cling onto Him.

 "Then he said, 'You skillfully sidestep God's law in order to hold on to your own tradition'" (Mark 7.9 NLT).

You are Beautiful

Sometimes I become so busy and self-absorbed that I forget the beauty of the people I care about. I overlook the immense respect that I have for my husband. I neglect the special connection I have with my sister.

I take for granted the love and joy I feel for my children. And I see past the sweet wisdom of my friend. Worst of all, I close my eyes to the majesty of my Heavenly Father.

But I am reminded. I am reminded by a song on the radio, the words of a believer and the glory of the sun-touched bay that God is awesome and all the earth sings His praises. He is beautiful, and He has created everything in this world to exclaim His glory. I close my eyes in shame and plead for God to forgive my selfishness.

How could I have forgotten His beauty? How could I have forgotten His Majesty? How could I have forgotten His love?

I pray that God reminds me every moment that He is good and His love for me is everlasting. I ask that He allow me to appreciate the beauty He sees in my husband, sister, children, friend and stranger.

I want my heart and eyes to focus through the lens of God's love, so that all that I see will be valuable to me. I am blessed to be a part of God's splendor, and I do not want to live life with eyes shaded by the ugliness of sin.

Though I will never fully understand the fullness of God's beauty, I pray that I can experience glimpses of it every day. I never want to take for granted the gratitude I have to be in His presence, living in His creation and forming relationships with His people.

"Honor the LORD for the glory of his name. Worship the LORD in the splendor of his holiness" (Psalm 29.2 NLT).

Whispered Amens

As my husband drove the babysitter home after our date night, I went upstairs to check on our son. Every night when I put him to sleep, I always pray over him. The prayers usually sound very similar:

"Father, thank You for allowing me to be Isaac's mommy. Thank You for all the wonderful activities we share together. Please put a hedge of protection around him while he sleeps. Help him to have the most beautiful and peaceful dreams. I pray that You fill his room with Your angels and glory and fill his heart with love, hope, peace and joy. Surround us with the love of Jesus Christ and the blood of His sacrifice. Forgive us of our mistakes and help us to make the right decisions for You. In Your name I pray, amen."

Every time I say the word, "amen," Isaac whispers his "amen," and I lay him in his bed.

On this particular night, however, the babysitter had already put Isaac in his bed and he was sound asleep. I put my hand on his tiny chest and I began the prayer that I've prayed over him all his life. He didn't budge or change his breathing.

When I finished, I whispered the word, "amen," and stared down at him for a moment with motherly love pouring from my face. A few seconds later, Isaac inhaled and a barely audible, "amen," floated from his lips.

He was deep asleep, yet repetition caused his two-year-old mind to subconsciously react to the prayer. I was amazed. Praying will be such a natural tendency in his life that he'll probably do it in his sleep.

"Start children off on the way they should go, and even when they are old they will not turn from it" (Proverbs 22.6 NIV).

The Good Lollipop

My son got a haircut at the salon, and since he did a great job, the hairstylist gave him a lollipop. She gave him a butterscotch one, which I have always hated. Inwardly, I was very upset with this lady. How dare she give my son the worst flavor lollipop. Did she not want to waste a good one (strawberry or watermelon) on my son?

After she gave him the lollipop, she squatted down to his level and gave him a big smile and said, "Butterscotch is my favorite flavor. I got that one just for you!"

Once she said that, I was simultaneously disappointed with myself and touched by the woman's thoughtfulness. She had chosen her favorite for my son. I had caught myself being self-focused again!

I needed to remember that my best and someone else's best may be two totally different things. I'm learning that people are going to do things for my family and me with the best intentions, and I need to stop looking through my own narrative to really understand where they are coming from.

I feel sometimes that we have become kings and queens of our own precious worlds, but I don't want that!

I would rather be a servant of God than a queen of my own opinions. My opinions are meaningless! I could have told that hairstylist to give my son a different flavor lollipop, but I would have robbed her of giving her best to my son.

I desire the best from others without the strangling strings of my own expectations. I pray that God will allow me to see past my viewpoint and to the good intentions of others.

"A fool finds no pleasure in understanding but delights in airing his own opinions" (Proverbs 18.2 NIV).

Spiritual Stains

Stains are everywhere. Just today I cleaned two kitty vomit stains, one potty training stain, two shirt stains and a bright pink stain on my handmade quilt. The work trying to salvage the stained items can become overwhelming. However, these are just the stains I allow myself to see.

I realize that there are many more stains from which I look the other way. Pen marks on the leather furniture, water stains on the wooden coffee table, spill stains on the car's upholstery, oil stains on the driveway and sun stains all over my body (freckles). I'm surrounded by stains! How could I possibly keep up with all of them?

This thought makes me think of my spiritual stains. I probably make more spiritual stains in one day then I make material stains in a year.

Does God ever tire of cleansing my spiritual stains? Do I show Him enough gratitude for caring so much for me? Do I allow God to cleanse me or do I hold onto my old stains?

I believe God takes pride in caring for His children, though sometimes we are ungrateful. God has created the most effective stain cleaner around: salvation!

He has given us the gift of salvation through Jesus Christ, which is the easiest and most effective way of cleansing us. Because of Christ, our stains are not only covered, but they are erased indefinitely.

When I think of the tiny material stains that surround my life, I am more appreciative of Christ's sacrifice and the love He shows us through His death on the cross. Keeping up with material stains may be overwhelming, but keeping up with spiritual stains would be impossible without Jesus.

 "Wash away all my iniquity and cleanse me from my sin" (Psalm 51.2 NIV).

Water Burden

It is spring, so I enrolled my kids in swim lessons. Since I have three kids, I played with two of them in the pool while the third was in a lesson. Each lesson was half an hour long, and I enjoyed the dynamics of having just two kids to interact with. While my middle child who is five was having his lesson, I had my three-year-old little girl clinging to me and my seven-year-old son splashing around me.

My seven-year-old loves to analyze, think, relate and communicate. He's like his mommy, except he would rather talk and I'd rather write. Apparently, he was enjoying my full attention because he spontaneously gave me a hug and said, "I love you, Mommy." He then wrapped his arms around me, and I held him gently with my free arm.

As I stood in the pool with my little girl in one arm and my oldest boy in the other, my analytical son said, "Wow, Mommy! The water helps you carry both of us!"

I instantly thought of the parallel of Jesus being our Living Water (John 4.10). Water has many amazing uses for the body, but I never thought of it as a way to lighten our load. Jesus tells us that if we connect ourselves to Him, our burdens would be easy to bear.

I used to struggle with this promise because my load always seemed so heavy. I would get frustrated because I knew I was missing out on a promise that was rightfully mine as a coheir with Christ and part of God's family. However, through years of doing life the wrong way, I've learned that when I keep my eyes centered on Christ, my load truly is easier.

Although there are short, difficult seasons in my life that strengthen my faith and resolve, I've found that for the most part each day feels like I'm being carried by the flow and ebb of Living Water. I've noticed that I have just enough time to do everything that God has called me to each day, especially spending time with Him.

I know that each person and journey is different; but as a woman, the main thing that burdened me was the opinions of others. I didn't realize how wide and deep my decisions, actions and emotions were affected by what I perceived other people thought. My load greatly lightened when I started to shed the clinging hands that I allowed to share my yoke with Christ.

I discovered the best way to lighten my load is to examine each of my thoughts, decisions and actions and see if it is yoked to Jesus or someone else. If I have unknowingly lassoed someone else's opinion into my actions, I quickly ask for forgiveness and release the burden. I have to be aggressive about not allowing others to replace God's authority and prominence in my life, because only He offers me buoyancy to carry on with ease.

"For my yoke is easy to bear, and the burden I give you is light" (Matthew 11.30 NLT).

Needy

Many years ago I went to a writers' conference, and for the first time my oldest son was without his mommy for five whole days. When I came back, he became extremely needy. He wanted my attention constantly. He ran to me when Daddy or Auntie tried to give him a hug (probably because they were the ones who watched him while I was gone). He wanted to be carried all of the time, which was difficult since I was eight months pregnant.

I would not allow myself to feel guilt or shame for my son's reaction because I knew that God wanted me to go on that trip. My son's odd behavior was his way of dealing with the fact that Mommy will not always be there for him (though, I wish that were possible). Finally, he assimilated back to his normal self, and he continued to ignore me for a toy or for Daddy once more.

My son's actions reminded me of my actions toward God. Sometimes I feel like God leaves me during difficult situations. When I was a new Christian, God always made His will apparently clear. I never had to consider my options because God held my hand and directed me through everything. However, now that I'm maturing as a follower of Christ, I sometimes feel less of His presence. I was very upset with Him at first. I wondered why He would leave me without any instruction.

However, I've come to realize that He wasn't leaving me; He was doing what any good father would do by allowing me to find my own way using the wits that He instilled in me. God expects more from me, and He desires for me to be a strong Christian able to make decisions based on what the Holy Spirit is teaching me. Now when I find myself in a difficult situation, I talk to God, rely on the Bible and take steps of faith.

I am honored that my Father would have so much faith in me! And if I do run into something that I can't handle, I'm confident that He'll pick me up before I fall and plant me back on His firm foundation again. I look forward to building confidence in my walk with Christ, and I can't wait until the day God can sit back, relax and watch His daughter run the course like a pro!

"'I will strengthen them in the Lord and in his name they will walk,' declares the Lord" (Zechariah 10.12 NIV).

A Mother's Sacrifice

I never knew how much sacrifice it would take to have children and to raise them. It's like our society sweeps the importance of being a mother under a rug. Being a mom just doesn't seem to be a big deal compared to a woman's appearance, her education or her resume.

I know as a youth, I took my mom for granted. But as I care for both my sons and daughter, I've come to appreciate my mom and all moms everywhere. Mothers really do rock! From the moment my first baby was conceived, my entire life became a living sacrifice: a physical, mental, emotional and spiritual sacrifice. And because of this, I am in awe of Jesus' sacrifice for us.

It's hard just having three kids; I can't imagine sacrificing myself for billions of people from the past, present and future. Talk about being emotionally and physically drained by the end of the day! And although I really can't comprehend the depth of Jesus' sacrifice for me, I want to tell Him daily that I appreciate what He did on the cross for my sins. I want to live my life in thankfulness for Jesus' sacrifice and my salvation.

I know the world sweeps what Jesus did for us under the rug too, but I'm determined not to. I want God and everyone to know that I love being a Christ-follower. My life is filled with unending hope, peace and love because I have been reconciled with God through Christ. I sacrifice gladly for my children knowing that Jesus died for them too.

"He is the atoning sacrifice for our sins, and not only for ours but also for the sins of the whole world" (1 John 2.2 NIV).

Hero or Dud

I knew two women with boyfriends who didn't want to commit. God asked both of these women to end their relationships. One woman ended the five-year relationship fully anticipating that her boyfriend would see the error of his ways and become the hero she wanted; instead, she was shocked when he agreed and six months later proposed to another woman and quickly started a family.

The second woman ended her five-year relationship with her boyfriend fully anticipating that he would agree and she would lose him forever. Her heart was broken, but she knew she deserved a hero, not a dud. When she told him that they needed to end the relationship, he wouldn't hear of it. He wanted to do whatever it would take to keep her. Suddenly, her dud became a hero.

Six months later he proposed to her. Both these stories seem different on the outset, but in actuality, they are exactly the same. Why? The first woman later found her hero, and they have been married for several years and have started a family. If this woman would have disobeyed God and waited on the dud, she would have lost the beautiful marriage and family she enjoys today.

The second woman, on the other hand, obeyed God allowing Him to un-shell her hero, and they have been married for several years and have also started their family. A hero as a husband is not some fantasy; it's Biblical. God says that a husband should be willing to die for his wife! How much more heroic can one get?

Although both husbands and wives will make mistakes along the way, they can continue their pursuit to encompass a Christ-like nature. If women are willing to be the Biblical wives that God has designed them to be, they can seek godly characteristics in their future husbands. And a couple who places Christ as the foundation of their marriage will be able to build a family together that shines the glory of God to the world.

"Husbands, love your wives, just as Christ loved the church and gave himself up for her" (Ephesians 5.25 NIV).

A Blessing for God

My husband and I were driving and talking about his job. He works in the medical field and serves people all day. And like most service-oriented jobs, it's easy to get burned out.

It is hard to work with people on a daily basis because people are not perfect: We are sometimes ungrateful, undeserving and unsatisfied.

Then I brought up a new topic. God has been doing so much for my husband and me and for our family that I really wanted to bless Him. I wanted to do something special just for God that He wasn't expecting.

"What can we do for God that would really bless Him?" I asked my husband. My husband then stated that Jesus said that when we serve others, we have served Him.

I thought about that for a moment, and I looked to the back seat of the car where both my sons were buckled up in their car seats. Then I realized something.

If someone wanted to give me a blessing, I would automatically say, "Don't give it to me. Give it to my sons." As a mother, I would find more joy in seeing my sons receive gifts than if I would receive them myself.

That is exactly what God wants from us. He wants us to bless each other—though, none of us is perfect. God is the ultimate father and He is blessed when we spread joy to His children. At that moment my question suddenly changed. I asked my husband, "What can we do for God's children, so we may be a blessing to God?"

"The King will reply, 'I tell you the truth, whatever you did for one of the least of these brothers of mine, you did for me'" (Matthew 25.40 NIV).

Essence of a Family

My family and I went water tubing with my brother's family. My six-year-old son rode on the jet ski with my brother as he pulled me on the tube. I told him that he would never knock me off the tube, which—come to find out—was the worst thing I could say.

My brother's sole ambition became to throw me off the tube.

I smiled every time I came to the surface after being slung into the water because I couldn't help but enjoy the thrill. I guess I must have smiled a lot because my son said he wanted to ride on the tube with me. I gave my brother the look, which said, "You better not knock off my son."

He looked at me and said, "Don't worry. I won't go fast."

My son got on the tube, and I put his hands on the two middle handles. I fastened my hands around him, and I tucked him under my body. His little face was just inches away from mine, and I could see him smiling the entire time. We skirted the waves, and the water splashed our faces, but we never went fast enough to be thrown off.

As we traveled around the lake, my son yelled, "Mommy! What

happens if I fall in the water?" I reached my face toward his ear and whispered, "If you fall, I will fall with you. We'll go into the water together."

As I said those words, I knew I had just captured the essence of family. Whether by blood, marriage, adoption or choice, a family creates life together. God supernaturally binds the unique purposes of each family member, so they become a beautiful praise offering to God.

"But Ruth replied, 'Don't urge me to leave you or to turn back from you. Where you go I will go, and where you stay I will stay. Your people will be my people and your God my God'" (Ruth 1.16 NIV).

The Sour Student

"A higher state of mind and spiritual vision can only be achieved through the higher practice of personal character. If you live up to the highest and best that you know in the outer level of your life, God will continually say to you, 'Friend, come up even higher.'" – Oswald Chambers: *My Utmost for His Highest*

I believe the hardest aspect about homeschooling is that your kids know you love them and that you would die for them; so they tend to take you, the teacher, for granted. There is no fear of the principal's office and no looming peer pressure to worry about. They can lay their self-centeredness and stubbornness on the table because, really, what's the worst thing that could happen?

As intimacy grows, fear and apprehension decrease. A comfortable, worry-free atmosphere becomes fertile soil for security, confidence and boldness; however, the weeds of arrogance, selfishness and laziness also sprout their wily roots. I stay busy plucking out the weeds of sin from my kids' lives while simultaneously protecting their beautiful growths of godliness. Needless to say, this mama is constantly grooming three amazing little gardens that are chock-full of potential.

I've also noticed that as my intimacy with Jesus deepens, I have to remember that He is the God of the Universe. Jesus is so profound and so awesome that no matter how comfortable I feel in my relationship with Him, there are intense parts of His nature that I have not experienced. I trust that I'm saved by grace and nothing can change that fact, but my salvation is just the beginning. Jesus is my Teacher, and He wants to teach me every day. He has a curriculum for my life and homework is mandatory.

I know how it feels to have complaining students dragging their feet to school every morning. And I always pray that my kids would have a better attitude and be excited to learn with me. But, here I am doing the same thing to my Teacher! I'm in a season of dragging my feet with Christ, finding it difficult to sit at the heavenly school table with Him. I don't want to give up sleep. I don't want to dig deeper in the Word. I don't want to do the busy work involved in learning from Him.

I groan and moan and justify my laziness with all the work I've already completed for Him. But God's not done with me yet. He wants to graduate me to the next level, but why should He when my attitude totally stinks? I've gotten so comfortable in the amazing grace of Christ that I've forgotten to fear my Lord. What an awesome privilege I have every day to learn from my Creator. I'm determined to give myself an attitude adjustment quickly, so my Teacher knows that I'm 100% excited and honored to be His student.

"O God, you have taught me from my earliest childhood, and I constantly tell others about the wonderful things you do" (Psalm 71.17 NLT).

Zipper

As I watched my five-year-old son try to zip up his jacket, I grew impatient. I had all the kids ready to get into the car, but he was holding up our exit. We were in our third minute of waiting when I asked, "Can I please zip it for you?" He kept his focus on his jacket and replied, "No. I want to do it by myself."

He was having trouble connecting the jacket zipper on the bottom, and I was tempted to just do that for him and let him zip it the rest of the way. But before I could reach down to help him, I had a flashback of my childhood. I distinctly remembered one morning when I was determined to zip up my own jacket. I saw myself standing in the hallway of my childhood home concentrating solely on that zipper. I don't remember how long it took me, but I know I was there for a while. I wouldn't budge until I figured it out!

Many times as Christians, we forget about the struggles we went through to gain the wisdom and skills that God desired for us. We see others who are smack-dab in the middle of a God-ordained teaching season, and we become impatient with them. We see them wrestling in an area that we have found victory, and we ridicule them or make them feel guilty. We become impatient and try to take over their valuable learning lesson. Even worse, we experience a "holier-than-thou" attitude and think that somehow we have "arrived" spiritually.

The truth of the matter is, however, we are all designed uniquely and have different backgrounds and upbringings that God is shaping and molding according to His timeline. Each of us will be held-up in a learning season during anointed moments on our path to heaven. When we extend to others the grace that Christ extends to us, we become holy cheerleaders. Let us remember that we are all fools that God has made wise.

"Do you see a man wise in his own eyes? There is more hope for a fool than for him" (Proverbs 26.12 NIV).

Heavenly Smiles

When I am holding my baby daughter, she gives everyone heavenly smiles. She is in my arms, and she feels the freedom to spread her sweetness to each new face that she sees. Her smiles melt the hearts of the passersby, and they always comment on how beautiful and sweet natured she is.

However, when my daughter leaves my arms, her sweetness completely disappears. When someone else is holding her, she frowns and cries and lets the whole world know her displeasure. She has no more heavenly smiles to give and no more sweetness to share. She is completely miserable and makes those around her anxious. Only when she is safely in my arms, does my daughter shine her sweet side again.

This is the same way with our Heavenly Father and us. When we diligently seek Him each day, it is easier to share love with others and look past offenses. If we have not sought God and we are trying to live on our own strength, we will fail miserably. Life is hard and people can hurt us, and many times it is easier to pass out frowns instead of smiles.

God calls us to love others as much as we love ourselves. That is impossible unless we are allowing God to fill us with His divine love. We can daily make an exerted effort to seek God and find strength in His arms. When we do, we'll be able to share heavenly smiles with those around us instead of frustrated frowns.

"He answered: 'Love the Lord your God with all your heart and with all your soul and with all your strength and with all your mind; and, love your neighbor as yourself'" (Luke 10.27 NIV).

Hiccup Distractions

I was driving in the car with my kids, and my oldest son who is six said that he had the hiccups. He was pretty upset over them and begged me for a remedy. Since I was driving and there's not much you can do for hiccups, I started telling him to do random things.

"Hold your breath, wave your arms and then yell as loud as you can," I said. He did this and nothing happened. "Look out the window and cough twenty times then stomp your feet for one minute." Again the hiccups came back. "Try to make yourself sneeze," I finally added, hoping that would distract him long enough to quiet his constant bellyaching from the backseat.

As my son tried to figure out how to sneeze, I wondered if that was how all the crazy remedies for the hiccups were created. A poor mother may have been in the middle of milking a cow, hemming a dress or plucking a chicken, and she needed some peace and quiet for a moment so she could concentrate. She'd tell her child to go drink from a cup backward. Her child—eager to get rid of the pesky hiccups—would run into the house for half an hour trying to figure out how not to spill water all over, hoping to quiet the spasms in his diaphragm.

Then I thought many Christians are doing that. The Enemy

distracts us with worries, pleasures and money in order to keep us away from our main purpose: Loving God and doing His will. I don't want to run around doing fruitless acts to fulfill the desires of my heart; I want to follow after God and fulfill the calling He has for me. I am determined not to allow myself to be distracted by the Enemy's schemes. It's impossible to drink from a cup backward!

"But the cares of this life let thorns come up. A love for riches and always wanting other things let thorns grow. These things do not give the Word room to grow so it does not give grain" (Mark 4.19 NLV).

Backseat Soul

I drive down the darkened street, allowing the thick, moist gulf breeze to fill my car. I glance up to see the image of my first-born in my rearview mirror. His smile reflects his soul—satisfied, replete, loved. His continuous flow of words depleted, and his heart overflows with gratitude, filling his emptied mind.

"Thank you, Mommy," he says more than once. "Thank you for spending time with me tonight."

I brought him grocery shopping with me. His history project suggested he explore the cereal aisle, examining the names of men who decided to reinvent breakfast with a creative spin on grain. I followed his endless string of words, while he maneuvered the mini-cart through the grocery store. I filled myself with his eager contemplations, and he greedily drank from my presence.

I had to surrender my worries to God; they fight to engulf the hollow space in my soul carved out for my son's infinite words.

I'm an imperfect substitute, role-modeling a relationship with our perfect Creator. One day I will be replaced, and my son's questions will veer from my ears to the Holy of Holies. I'm cognizant that my position as my son's adoration is finite. I will sap my strength to push his abilities beyond mine, so God will have a loyal prince in the service of the Most High.

But everything begins with a sacrificial love: A love of a mother laying down her life for just one. That kind of love is immovable, and unleashes the power of every kind of good: trust, faithfulness, loyalty, grace, confidence, boldness, security, power and purpose. All these traits are required to change the world for Christ, and I don't want him struggling with them as an adult, like his mother.

Every seed of greatness is buried in the fertile soil of tedium. So I will walk down the aisles of life and gather every syllable of my son's inquisitions. In heaven, I will count each one like precious jewels and regret the ones I allowed to slip from my eternal reward.

I wish my car could linger in this moment. My son whispers the same sentiment from the backseat. I stick my arm into the black layers of night, and the dense wind pulls at my hand, pleading for me to open my eyes. My car speakers fill the saturated air with songs of praise, glorifying a Living God. I finally notice the palm trees bowing to His majesty and the wind dancing in exultation throughout creation. And I'm left with an undeniable Truth: Even the kings of this world will bow to the Son of Man.

"Yea, all kings shall fall down before him: all nations shall serve him" (Psalm 72.11 KJV).

Enthusiasm Outshines

My six-year-old son started playing soccer. He doesn't quite know what he's doing and the rules are a bit confusing to him, but he has stellar passion and enthusiasm for the game. His smile stays fixed on his face; and when he or his teammate makes a good play, he cheers and hollers. His passion spreads to the other teammates and his coach. They all get excited over seemingly simple moves. This passion—placed in him by a family that continuously exposes his significance—gives him power and strength to play hard and overcome his limitations and lack of skill.

When I see my son play, I think of the servant who was given five talents (Matthew 25.14-30). He was given more than the other two servants according to his abilities. I always believed that the servant was given more talents because he was more skilled; however, I know that skill does not necessarily ensure a person's productivity. When you read the end of the parable, you find that the Master does not become upset because of the one-talent servant's lack of ability; rather, it was the servant's laziness that angered the Master.

When I researched the word ability, I discovered that it means something very different. The Greek word for ability is *dynamis*, which means power. It is the same word used to illustrate the power that surged through Jesus' body when the woman from the crowd touched his clothes and was healed (Mark 5.30). Dynamis has little to do with a person's skill-set but has everything to do with the power residing in the person. That power comes from the Holy Spirit who lives in Christians once we have the covering of Jesus' righteousness.

We as Christians all have the power of the Holy Spirit residing in us, but it stays untapped until our passion for Christ unleashes it. When our actions follow our passion, we can accomplish anything that God has for us. We don't have to be skilled or smart. In fact, God says that He uses foolish things to confound the wise (1 Corinthians 1.27). We just have to want to be used by the Holy Spirit, want to do more for the Kingdom of God, want to be endowed with more responsibility. We need to WANT more of Him!

The coach put my son in the game not because he's a skilled player, but because my son wants to play. His passion usurps his ability. I believe if we all fully understood the significance that God places on us, we too would be passionate about His plan for our lives. And instead of being content with just one or two talents, we would beseech more from the Master. We might not have the amazing abilities that others have; but what we lack in ability, we make up for in enthusiasm.

"I came to you in weakness with great fear and trembling. My message and my preaching were not with wise and persuasive words, but with a demonstration of the Spirit's power, so that your faith might not rest on human wisdom, but on God's power" (1 Corinthians 2.3-5 NIV).

Paul himself was scared to do the things of God, but he did not let that stop him. He relied on the Spirit of God inside of him to accomplish God's mighty work. Paul's life is an amazing example of living with the power of the Holy Spirit. Paul might not have been the most eloquent speaker, but he wanted to be used by God. He was passionate about running a good race, and he was obviously a five-talent servant. We all can be five-talent servants if we are passionate for God and His Kingdom.

Applesauce

My middle son was having a bad day. It seemed that nothing would go his way—according to his six-year-old mindset. I tried everything to bless, encourage and strengthen him. I decided to prepare a candlelight dinner in the formal dining room to help boost his mood. The extra effort to light the candles, provide the cloth napkins and eat on the fancy dinnerware pours greatly into all my kids.

After our meal, I offered applesauce to my kids unaware that I only had one portion size left. My four-year-old daughter was the first to meet me at the refrigerator, so I handed the cup to her and explained to my boys that they could have yogurt. My middle son had run behind his sister, trying to claim the applesauce first; and he crumpled to the ground when he saw her walk back to the table with it. Then he began to cry.

I knew his day had been difficult, and I desperately wanted another container of pink strawberry flavored applesauce for my heartbroken son to magically appear. Suddenly, I remembered seeing apples in the refrigerator when I went looking for the strawberries that I served my kids for lunch. Plus, I knew that there were a few strawberries still left in the container.

I knelt down next to my son and asked him if he would like to make homemade strawberry applesauce. Instantly, his countenance changed, and he quickly got off the floor. I sliced up the apples and strawberries, and my son put them in the blender and pushed the medium speed button. Two minutes later, I poured homemade applesauce into three beautiful glass bowls and watched as my kids happily ate their dessert.

My middle son's face lit up with joy, and I became aware of how much God loves my boy. God knew this day would happen. He knew that my son's little heart would be sad, so He made sure that two apples and a few strawberries would be left in the refrigerator for this moment. And I'm reminded that my efforts as a mother will always fall short, and that is why I claim the power, strength, peace, wisdom, gentleness, understanding and the abundance of the Holy Spirit in my life.

I can rest in the Holy Spirit's leading as a mother because I know that He desires God's best for my family.

"So if you sinful people know how to give good gifts to your children, how much more will your heavenly Father give the Holy Spirit to those who ask him" (Luke 11.13 NLT).

A Sticker and a Whisper

As I sat in church before the music started, I looked down at my whitewashed denim jeans. A two-inch square sticker with a combination of letters and numbers clung to my pants just above my knee. This piece of insignificant paper represented my three children who were enjoying children's church and learning about Jesus. I would need to give this sticker to the children volunteers in order to collect my lovely little ones after the service.

My eyes would travel down to this sticker every now and then during the one hour of worship and preaching, and I found it ironic that such a feeble thing could possibly symbolize the little souls that I would sacrifice my life to love, care for and protect.

The comparison between the lives entrusted to me and the label on my jeans was laughable; yet, the system of dropping off and picking up kids was necessary for establishing a safe and peaceful environment for both the parents and children at church.

Without this system, church would be chaotic and very little learning and growth would occur. Everything that produces something of significance (relationships, family, home, work, government and life) must have an established system in place for positive movement to occur.

As I stared at my sticker, I thought of the prayer of salvation that I whispered when I was fifteen years old. Two college students came to our small youth group one weekend and led a little revival. I don't know exactly what I said, but I know that something supernatural was opened in my life. My words were feeble and insignificant, yet they unlocked the most beautiful and amazing gift available to all of us: An intimate relationship with our Creator.

Many people have difficulty entering into a relationship with God because they can't grasp how simple the system of salvation is. Before all the theology theory and religious discourse, there is simply a need—a need for meaning, significance, purpose, love, forgiveness, wholeness and truth. There is a person who sits up one day and realizes that there has to be more to life than living and dying. And whether they confess this need with the mouth of their body, mind or spirit; God takes hold of this symbolic whisper and opens the doors of His grace, favor, love, forgiveness and Spirit.

Jesus did all the work. All we need to do is believe and receive.

"If you openly declare that Jesus is Lord and believe in your heart that God raised him from the dead, you will be saved" (Romans 10.9 NLT).

Closed Hibiscus Bloom

My daughter loves to pick me flowers. I have to watch her as we walk our church's lawn, because she will pick the beautifully landscaped flower bushes along the way. I have taught her that she can't pick flowers outside our gym, neighbor's house or at the store. But at home, she is able to pick flowers to her heart's content.

Since spring has begun, she has brought me several sweet bouquets of wild flowers from a nearby field and cultured flowers from our hibiscus bushes. One day I was sitting at my computer typing, and my daughter came in with two huge hibiscus flowers.

The broad blossoms wore a brilliant scarlet shade and their petals opened wide like soup bowls. They adorned my plain brown desk with a cheerful touch of the warmer season. I glanced at them every now and then, recalling little images of my daughter's precious face and letting my love for her simmer into my awareness.

When I came back to my desk later that night, I couldn't believe how much my crimson blooms had changed. Instead of opened and brilliant, they had become dull and narrow. Each teardrop petal had folded inward, until the entire blossom had transformed into an unnoticeable, thin piece of organic material.

The metamorphosis that took place in only a few short hours was disheartening, and I couldn't believe the pitiful flowers on my desk were the same vivid ones that my daughter had gifted me earlier.

The Holy Spirit whispered to me, "That's what happens to my children when they disconnect from me."

When we stay rooted in God, our lives are wide open and receptive to Him. We absorb all His goodness and share the luster of His glory wherever we go. However, if we disconnect from His presence and purpose, we begin to focus on ourselves. Our lives fold inward into selfishness and pride, and we lose sight of the greater meaning of our existence.

It is far too easy to push off spending time with God and His Word. Life gets busy and daily responsibilities take precedence. Before we know it, we have become so self-focused that we've forgotten to stay sensitive to the Holy Spirit. The Fruit of the Spirit shrivels, and we wonder why we have lost our peace, joy and hope.

But unlike the closed hibiscus, we can tap back into God's abundance at any time. Our bloom can reopen to the Holy Spirit, and our lives will once again produce spiritual fruit. Life is too valuable to waste it away as a closed hibiscus bloom. Taking time each day to spend with God will keep our lives radiant and meaningful, and we will add a touch of His splendor to the world around us.

"The wilderness and the wasteland shall be glad for them, and the desert shall rejoice and blossom as the rose" (Isaiah 35.1 NKJV).

The Burden of Blessings

When my son was in kindergarten, I talked about two parakeets my family owned when I was a child. I pulled from my memory to describe their beautiful colors, their ability to repeat several words and their willingness to perch on my finger. I painted such an amazing picture of my childhood birds that my son desperately wanted to get his own winged pets.

My son decided to save up his allowance, so he could buy two birds, a cage, food and bird toys. It took him about a year and a half to earn the money, but he did it! He beamed with pride and excitement when carried his little cage, housing his two bright pet birds, into our home. I was so thrilled that he would experience the same joy I remembered from raising birds as a girl.

About two weeks later, the reality of how much work birds require dawned on me. Birds have to be fed and watered constantly and their cage has to be cleaned every week. They are fun pets, but they create a mess of seeds, feathers and waste all around them. Somehow, the work involved with caring for the birds slipped my memory, and I realized very quickly that the burden of owning birds was a lot for my seven-year-old son.

I talked to my older sister about our childhood birds, and she laughed! She said that we never owned them. We had only bird-watched them for a few weeks. No wonder I had such a one-sided view of caring for them. I had only experienced the blessing of birds without the burden of the responsibility.

Sometimes God protects us from diving head-first into our one-sided, idealized viewpoints. With every blessing comes a greater amount of responsibility, and we must ensure that our capacity can handle the stretching of our borders. Many times we look at people who have what we want, but we don't fully understand the sacrifices they are making in the background of their lives. Once we experience the full weight of the responsibility, our romanticized opinions may lose their luster.

God has designed each of us so differently, and our abilities are tailored to the dreams and desires He has placed in our hearts. When we find ourselves desiring another person's blessings, we need to decide if the burden of those blessings fits into the uniqueness of our personalities. Has God given us the grace for the grind? Plus, we have to be honest with ourselves about our capacity. If we complain about the borders of our responsibilities now, how could we handle those borders expanding?

Humility is the best cure for these one-sided, idealized viewpoints. As we humble ourselves, we gain an adequate understanding of our strengths and weaknesses and a truer perception of our intentions. We may lose our interest in something if we knew the work involved outweighed the satisfaction gained. Or we may discover that we have been motivated by self-glory instead of God's glory. We might actually find ourselves thankful that God has given the blessing and burden to someone else, so we can be free to turn our attention to the blessings and burdens God has designed specifically for our lives and purpose.

"Because of the privilege and authority God has given me, I give each of you this warning: Don't think you are better than you really are. Be honest in your evaluation of yourselves, measuring yourselves by the faith God has given us" (Romans 12.3 NLT).

Give Me, Give Me

I've recently made a habit of waking up early and praying in a certain room of my house. This room is far away from my bedroom, so I won't be tempted to fall back asleep. I turn off the alarm (for the second or third time) and shuffle to my little prayer niche, and I melt away from the world into a timeless place with God.

All too quickly, though, I hear little voices on the other side of the door. My two youngest kids (ages three and six) are awake, and they begin to bring me back to reality and to the burdens and blessings of my time on earth.

I call for them to come in, and they quickly jump onto my lap to snuggle with their mom. One particular morning, my six-year-old son was still angry from the night before. His sister got the toy he wanted from the restaurant toy vending machine, and his mind was fixated on it.

Instead of being able to hold him and tell him how much I love him and how valuable he is to me, the room was filled with his complaints, petitions and reminders concerning this particular toy. I became irritated because his mind was so focused on what he wanted that I couldn't bless him with my words of love, comfort, peace, joy and purpose.

As I listened to him continue, God pointed out to me: "This is what you have done in the past."

God had given me some beautiful promises; but instead of confidently waiting for His timing, I complained, petitioned and reminded God nonstop for years. Every moment I had alone with God, I would use it up with my voice ringing out my discontent.

I believe that we are supposed to keep our eyes on our vision, and I know that God likes it when we confess the desires of our hearts; but when we focus more on the promise than the Promise Giver, we have become out of balance.

I wonder how many life-giving words I missed out on because I couldn't hear them over my own loud murmuring.

There is nothing wrong with longing for God's promises, but we must learn to wait with confidence in His faithfulness. God is producing a special purpose for each of us, and we need to be patient until the work is complete; so His glory will rest thickly in our minds, hearts, lives and destinies.

One of my pastors always asks me: "How do you spell faith?"

And the answer is always the same: "W A I T."

Let us be determined to fall in love with all that God is doing in our lives and listen to His sweet life-giving words for us. Our goals and promises may still feel a long way off; but instead of complaining, let us focus on how much God loves us. He loves us so much that He came into our broken world to set us free from our sin, so we could spend eternity with Him. Now THAT gift deserves a little "Give me, Give me!"

"Wait patiently for the LORD. Be brave and courageous. Yes, wait patiently for the LORD" (Psalm 27.14 NLT).

The Wrong Wedding Cake

Planning my wedding was difficult for me. My family was far away, and I had never organized anything beyond a small birthday party. I received a lot of help from friends, pointing me in the right direction. Since I was a senior in college and lived off of my waitressing tips, I was on a tight budget. One friend gave me the number of a local lady who baked cakes from her home. I went to her house and flipped through her cake magazines, and I finally found the cake of my dreams.

My spring wedding was going to be held in a charming garden, so I wanted a cake with large, frosted flowers and leaves draping down one side of the stacked tiers of round cakes. My chosen cake was very plain and simple besides the colorful foliage made out of frosting. I was very pleased that I had actually picked something that would fit the feel of my reception, and I looked forward to the display of edible flowers on my special cake.

The day of my wedding, the bridesmaids came early to the garden area outside of the reception hall to take pictures. My friends were decked out like lavender cupcakes, and we enjoyed the creativity of the photographer (also a friend of one of my friends). I was in awe of how God had brought all the details together. There was no way in my financial situation and wedding planning ignorance that

I would have been able to pull off such a beautiful and memorable wedding.

A friend came by and told me that my wedding cake had arrived and the baker was waiting to talk with me. As I walked into the reception hall, I knew right away that the cake was nothing like I ordered it. The lady waited for me as I looked over the cake. It had the plain white-tiered cakes; but instead of large frosted flowers and leaves gracefully flowing down my cake, each tier was topped with a small bundle of faux lavender flowers.

I stared at the cake for several moments, while the woman who brought the cake stared at me. Finally, I came to a conclusion.

"It looks beautiful," I said.

The woman looked relieved and quickly grabbed her things and left.

I walked to my dressing room and waited for my groom to arrive. My sister asked me how I liked the cake, and I told her that it wasn't what I ordered but it was okay. I wouldn't let something small ruin my whole day. The beauty of what God had done for me that day overshadowed my insignificant and subjective opinion on cake design.

Many of us want God to do great things in our lives, but we micro-manage the details. However, when God performs a miracle, the details will be too numerous and too overwhelming for us to control. God will orchestrate something beautiful and meaningful in our lives, but we must allow people to have their opinions, their methods, and their mistakes. There are infinite ways to accomplish a single goal, and we can have complete confidence that God will achieve His perfect plan through the creative minds of others.

Nothing eternally beautiful can be made without the involvement of the Holy Spirit. So instead of sweating the details, we should be praying and seeking God's Spirit to demonstrate His power, glory and grace in our lives, families, ministries, churches, events, etc. And we need to give freedom to those around us to have their own beautiful subjectiveness. We can trust that God will establish His presence in every detail done in His name. When we let go of trying to control every little thing, we will gain freedom to enjoy the breathtaking wedding that God is orchestrating on our behalf between His son and His Bride, the Church.

"Let us be glad and rejoice, and let us give honor to him. For the time has come for the wedding feast of the Lamb, and his bride has prepared herself" (Revelation 19.7 NLT).

Peace Replaced Flinches

"I am leaving you with a gift—peace of mind and heart. And the peace I give is a gift the world cannot give. So don't be troubled or afraid" (John 14.27 NLT).

Our mini-dachshund, Rusty, was gifted to us just over a year ago. When he came into our home, he behaved timidly and flinched at all of our moves to pet and hold him. Understandably, he missed his mom and his first home. Our family was new to him, and he didn't know how to behave or what to expect.

A couple of weeks ago, Rusty—now full-grown—leisurely slept on a futon, which is located next to my work out weights. After I lifted each set of weights, I would place the heavy load onto the futon. Rusty was several feet away from where I set the weights, but the mattress still shook a little each time.

I noticed that he didn't even bat an eye when I laid the 15-pound weights down, but I thought for sure he would want to know what was going on when I placed both 35-pound weights down together! Nope. He didn't flinch. He merely yawned, stretched and rolled onto his side.

Here are weights that could crush him with one blow, but he

continued snoozing like he had nothing to worry about.

I realized that over the course of a year, Rusty not only learned to adjust to our family, but he learned to trust us with his life. When the kids pick him up, he merely waits for them to get bored and put him back down. When someone accidently lays on him, he peeks his head out and squeezes his way to freedom—never once does he look worried or distraught.

Even when my husband has to take him a bath or remove a thorn from his skin, Rusty—although looking uncomfortable—doesn't try to jump or bark. He has learned that our family loves him and only wants the best for him. He trusts us even in painful situations.

As Christians develop a deeper relationship with Christ, we stop flinching in hard situations and start relying on and trusting in God. There is a peace attainable to all of us when we understand that God loves us and only wants the best for us. This peace is foreign to the world void of Christ; and when we demonstrate this peace even in the midst of a storm, the world will notice and wonder why we are different.

In difficult times, we can continue to trust God even when we don't understand, believing and claiming that His plans are always for our good.

"For I know the plans I have for you," declares the LORD, "plans to prosper you and not to harm you, plans to give you hope and a future" (Jeremiah 29.11 NIV).

Making Beds

"For the sin of this one man, Adam, caused death to rule over many. But even greater is God's wonderful grace and his gift of righteousness, for all who receive it will live in triumph over sin and death through this one man, Jesus Christ" (Romans 5.17 NLT).

Occasionally, I would tell my kids to make their beds. I feel like a tidy bed is just the thing to slip into every night after a full day. My boys did the best they could to align the sheets, quilt and pillow; but it was obvious that they didn't take too much care into the process. I wasn't consistent about enforcing the bed-making standard, so their understanding and appreciation of it hadn't been developed.

One morning, I decided to make their beds for them. I went to each of my three kids' rooms, and neatly arranged their bedclothes. It took me only a few minutes to sweep through their rooms with an organized hand, and I felt a sense of love for my two sons and daughter as I straightened their crumpled blankets.

I enjoyed this morning process so much that I continued to do it each day, except for Saturday. Saturday is my day of rest and the day my kids sleep in. There is no school the next day, so I let the beds stay in their unkempt, weekend state. However, after about a month of making their beds, I noticed that my sons started making it themselves Saturday night right before bed. They had become so accustomed to the standard of a nicely made bed that they were willing to make the bed themselves to keep this standard.

I watched as my kids carefully arranged their sheets, quilt and pillow to the exact location that I place them every morning. They even turned down the top sheet and blanket like I had the habit of doing for them. In all the time I started making their beds, I never asked them to make it themselves. But here they were initiating a bed cleaning session on their own!

During this same time, I had been struggling with the truth that I am the righteousness of Christ. I'd hear the words and understand them, but I knew my actions weren't reflecting this belief. I still chased after righteousness (right-standing with God) like it could be achieved, even though I understood that I could never have righteousness on my own (Romans 3.28 NIV).

One night I wrestled with God, and I opened up about hidden behaviors that were not rooted in Truth. I told Him that I was always trying to be good enough in His eyes. I constantly analyzed my thoughts, words and actions; eager to change so God would find me worthy to bless. I felt like I was chasing righteousness instead of living in it.

Then God reminded me of my kids' beds. My kids did not claim the tidy-bed standard until they saw their beds made every day (minus Saturdays) for several weeks. They had to slip into wonderfully neat beds every night for them to begin to appreciate and embrace this standard. And once they became accustomed to that standard, they made actions toward keeping and promoting it. They began living in this new standard on their own.

By grace God has freely given us His standard of righteousness, but many Christians don't live in this standard because they haven't fully embraced it. They either don't completely grasp the profound fact that they are blameless before a perfect God or they are stuck, like I was, in the vicious cycle of chasing after righteousness. But we are the righteousness of Christ—all of our past, present and future mistakes are hanging on a cross, buried in the tomb and swallowed up in Christ; and we are dead to their sting (1 Corinthians 15.55-57).

The world's way is backward in God's Kingdom. Instead of telling people to act righteously, we need to tell them that they ARE righteous in Christ over and over again until they believe it (2 Corinthians 5.21). And once people embrace the standard of righteousness that was given to them freely, they will start living righteously—not because they have to but because they have adopted that standard as their own! When we start acting righteously because we believe ourselves to be righteous, our actions and faith will work together to demonstrate to the world our belief in Jesus Christ (James 2.22).

"Yet we know that a person is made right with God by faith in Jesus Christ, not by obeying the law. And we have believed in Christ Jesus, so that we might be made right with God because of our faith in Christ, not because we have obeyed the law. For no one will ever be made right with God by obeying the law" (Galatians 2.16 NLT).

Disobedient Driver

I was driving in the car with my oldest son who is five years old. He and I were going grocery shopping together. As I drove, he was telling me all about what he learned at Sunday school. I stopped at a stop sign then continued driving down the street, and my son said from the back seat, "Mommy, you are so obedient."

This made me smile. My husband and I have been trying to teach our son about obedience. We tell him that we're teaching him to obey us so that one day he'll know how to obey God. God will be able to bless his life only when he is obedient to God's direction.

I wondered what obedience my son saw in me. Did he notice how I try to always keep the house clean so my family can have a peaceful home? Did he see me volunteer for our church and understand the sacrifice I made? Or did he watch me take time out of my busy schedule to read the Bible and talk with God?

What my son said took me by surprise. He said, "You are obedient when you drive. You don't break the rules so that the police officers don't pull you over."

After he said that, I had to take my foot off of the gas. I was driving faster than the speed limit and, thereby, breaking the law.

My son's perceptions of my obedience even in the smallest of circumstances made me realize how important it is to obey the laws—God's laws and man's laws. My son notices every little thing I do, and he can sniff out a double standard instantly.

How can I teach my son the importance of obedience when I'm disregarding laws that I don't really care for? I'm sure my son doesn't care for a dozen rules that I enforce (brushing his teeth, washing his hands, picking up his toys), but he still has to do them for his own good.

I want to model to my son how to obey the rules out of love. I don't want him to see me obeying the laws because of some guilt-trip or out of legalistic duty. I want to obey the laws out of respect and love for my God. I want my son to see my obedience in every facet of my life—not because I have to obey but because I want to obey. As long as the laws correspond with the Bible and are for "my own good," I should strive for obedience.

If I want my son to obey and brush his teeth when I ask him to, I better take my foot off the gas and slow down!

"The fear of the Lord is pure, enduring forever. The decrees of the Lord are firm, and all of them are righteous. They are more precious than gold, than much pure gold; they are sweeter than honey, than honey from the honeycomb" (Psalm 19.9-10 NIV).

Lonely Water Slides

My second-born son loves going on lone adventures—riding his bike, sliding down a water slide, exploring a new trail, etc.—but the only problem is that he doesn't like to do them alone. Being a middle child (two years younger than his brother and two years older than his sister), he is used to having people around. So when he wants to take on a solo project, he becomes torn between his desire to dive in and his fear of being alone.

I usually become his playmate when he does something new. I've run full speed in my flip-flops next to my son while he navigated his first few trips on a new bike because he wouldn't ride it otherwise. I've scrambled down a medium water slide fully dressed in order to reach my son who had lodged himself in the middle of the yellow tube, screaming for me to come with him. I've traveled the short distance of our backyard with my son who wasn't comfortable to play by himself until he had investigated the entire perimeter with me.

I love being there for my son, but I know that I won't be able to journey with him on every path God leads him down.

I think many times we don't obediently follow God into the unknown because we are scared. We pray for God to bring us a helper, an encourager, a fellow traveler; however, as our faith becomes stronger, God will limit the hand-holding people around us. Sometimes we will find ourselves alone at a very scary fork in the road, and we may feel that God is neglecting or abandoning us.

Is God being insensitive to our feelings? No.

God is the only One who completely understands us and unconditionally loves us, which is demonstrated by God sending His Son to die for us on the cross. He knows the number of hairs on our heads (Luke 12.7) and the hidden thoughts of our hearts (Psalm 139.2). And He wants us to learn to depend on the movement of His Spirit, while putting our faith in Jesus and our trust in His Word, the Bible. God desires to be our "playmate" in life—the One we turn to first, the One we rely on most, the One we want to journey with us.

In my experience, God will limit the comfort and assurance we find in people because He wants us to find true comfort and assurance in Him. The Holy Spirit lives in us, Jesus prays for us and the Bible guides us. There will come a time when we must choose to walk blindly into God's will, confidently putting all of our hopes, fears and dreams into His sovereign hands. When we go on those lone adventures and take on those solo projects despite our fears of being alone, we show God that we truly believe He is doing life with us. We are never alone.

"Do you not know that you are God's temple and that God's Spirit dwells in you?" (1 Corinthians 3.16 ESV).

Do You Love Me Most?

My oldest son sat at the kitchen table looking down at his folded hands. I was preparing Sunday lunch, and I could tell that he was thinking.

He's probably reflecting on his morning at children's church, I mused.

My son finally looked up at me and said, "You don't love me most, do you, Mommy?"

His question stopped me. "Of course, I love you. I would die for you."

He looked back down again. "Yes, but you don't love me most."

I quickly washed my hands and shook them dry as I walked to the table and sat down next to him.

"What do you mean?" I asked, wanting to know specifically what thoughts were coursing through his brain.

"You are supposed to love God most, so that means you don't love me most," he said. Red outlined his eyes and tears began to trace his cheeks.

I knew that he must have learned about loving God at church. We are called to love Him most, which is a difficult topic to understand, especially for a seven-year-old.

"Loving God most doesn't mean I love you any less," I said taking his hand. "In fact, loving God most allows me to love you even more."

He looked up at me shaking his head in frustration. "How?"

"My love for God makes me want to be a better mommy, to be a better wife to Daddy and to be a better friend to others. It's hard to explain but when my heart loves God, He gives me more love to share."

"But why are we supposed to love God most?" he asked, becoming more upset.

"Because without God, I wouldn't have you," I answered.

My son's face relaxed a bit. "What do you mean?"

"God created this world. He created Daddy and me. And He created you and your brother and sister. Without God, nothing would exist. I love Him because He gave me my family," I said, hoping my son's young mind would understand.

"So if there wasn't a God, where would I be?" my son asked as his inquisitive mind explored the possibilities.

"You wouldn't be here," I answered.

"Where would I be?" he asked again.

"You wouldn't be anywhere," I said. "God created everything, so without Him nothing would exist."

"I would be dead," he asked, struggling to comprehend the absence of God.

"No, you would have never been born. None of us would have been born. This earth, the moon, the sun, people—all of life would be empty."

My son contemplated my words, and I saw a spark of understanding. I could tell he felt better, but I knew the shift from self-love to God-love would take time. I pulled his hand and took him into my arms.

"I know you love me very much," I whispered in his ear. "Someday, though, you will love God more. But your love for me now is teaching you how to love God when you're older. And as your love for God grows, you'll be able to love me even more."

"You love him even though you have never seen him. Though you do not see him now, you trust him; and you rejoice with a glorious, inexpressible joy" (1 Peter 1.8 NLT).

The Walking Dead

"He said to him, 'If they do not listen to Moses and the Prophets, they will not be convinced even if someone rises from the dead'" (Luke 16.31 NIV).

"I want to ask you something, Mommy," my eight-year-old son said from the backseat of our SUV.

"What's up?" I asked.

He hesitated. "Huh, never mind."

When my son becomes wary about asking a question, I know that it is important. "Why don't you ask me at home."

"Okay," he said.

There were a lot of people with us and the car ride home was noisy. I knew he was struggling with something, so I wanted to make sure that we were alone and the atmosphere was quiet before we talked about it.

When we got home, he led me to his room and opened his Bible to his reading from the day before. "Why doesn't Abraham let Lazarus warn the Rich Man's brothers about hell?" He finally asked. "I thought the Holy Spirit wants to forgive us."

I read Luke 16.19-31 with my son. It was the story about Lazarus and the Rich Man—not quite a parable because Jesus uses a person's name (the same name of a friend He literally raises from the dead).

"Why is the Holy Spirit not forgiving the people? I thought the Holy Spirit loves us!" my son said, obviously upset.

I paused for a second, considering my words. I knew this was a special moment. "Jesus died for everyone's sins, and the Holy Spirit wants all of us to receive salvation. But we must choose to accept it."

He still looked confused.

I continued. "If I bought you a gift, but you refused to take it, would you have it?"

He thought. "No."

"No, you wouldn't. You must accept the gift for it to be yours. The Holy Spirit offers Jesus' sacrifice to the rich and the poor, but they must choose to receive it," I said, hoping he would understand my metaphor.

"But why wouldn't Abraham let Lazarus come back from the dead? If people saw him, they would believe and be saved."

"No, people still wouldn't believe," I answered.

"How do you know?" he asked.

"Because God came into this world in the form of Jesus and died for our sins, experiencing separation from God Himself! Jesus then came back to earth three days later, and over 500 people saw Him (1 Corinthians 15.6). Jesus told all His disciples to tell everyone around the world that He died and came back to life to save us. But you know what?"

"What?" he asked with his eyes wide.

I leaned forward and whispered. "People still didn't believe Him. Jesus died and came back to life to warn us about a big chasm that separates us from God, but many people did not accept His gift of salvation (Luke 16.26). Jesus loves all of us, and He took all of our sins and gave all of us His righteousness. But many people will not accept the gift. And when they die, they cannot be born into the presence of God because they are not perfect like Jesus. They are born on the other side of the chasm, which we call hell, but it simply means the absence of God."

"Why can't we be perfect?" he asked.

"Because God gave us free will to choose, and sometimes we choose to do things that are wrong. But Jesus took our mistakes and gave us His perfection. And guess what?" I asked.

"What?"

"All we have to do is accept Jesus' perfection as our own. It's a free gift."

"But I can't see the gift. How do I know it's real?" he asked.

"Can you see my love for you?"

"No," he said.

"Then how do you know my love for you is real?"

He sat quietly.

"It's called faith. You believe it without seeing it. That's what we do for Jesus' gift of salvation—we believe even though we can't see it. We are made righteous not when we are perfect, but when we believe by faith!"

"I wish Jesus would just hurry up and come back again," my son said.

"Not yet," I said. "There's still time."

"Time for what, Mommy?" he asked.

"There's time to tell everyone that our Creator became human and died and came back to life, so that when we are born into eternity, we will be in heaven where God is. We must tell everyone about Jesus because He loves all His children and He wants us all to spend eternity with Him. That's why we are here: to bring as many people with us to heaven as possible. Jesus is the only way."

"What will heaven be like?" he asked, getting excited.

"I don't know, but it will be pretty cool!"

"For God so loved the world that he gave his one and only Son, that whoever believes in him shall not perish but have eternal life. For God did not send his Son to condemn the world, but to save the world through him. Whoever believes in him is not condemned, but whoever does not believe stands condemned already because they have not believed in the name of God's one and only Son" (John 3.16-18 NIV).

The Blessing Box

I play a simple game with my kids that they really enjoy. I love this game because it is easy for someone like me who is creatively challenged when it comes to crafts and games for kids. All you have to do is get a medium-sized box and cut a hole in it large enough to fit a kid's hand. Then you go around the house and grab 10-15 items and put them in the box. The kids then each take their turn closing their eyes, reaching into the box, grabbing something and guessing what it is.

It's amazing to watch the kids as they behold their treasure. It might be a bottle of whiteout, an eraser, a quarter, a straw or swim goggles; but they are completely mesmerized by it. They feel it in their tiny palms—their minds working hard to identify it—and when they open their eyes, they are surprised and excited by what they've discovered.

During this game, they place great value onto an item that they normally take for granted or don't even notice. They become aware of its importance and function in their lives and our family. What I found interesting is that those items don't even make up a tiny fraction of what we own. Our house is full of thousands of little items that can be singled out and placed into a box.

While playing this game, I explained to the kids the value of appreciating what God has given us. If we truly understand how blessed we are, we wouldn't find ourselves in covetous discontent. Plus, if we look eye-to-eye at each and every one of our blessings, we would see its worth and rise up to be the good stewards God called us to be; and we would come away with the unmistakable understanding that we are rich with God's bounty.

Without even looking at the material possessions in our home, we can focus on the relationships God has blessed us with. No matter what is happening in our circumstances or how rich or poor we think we are, the fact that we have a spirit and the One who created that spirit loves us is pretty awesome. The free gift of eternal life in heaven with God bought for us by the sacrifice of Jesus Christ overshadows anything we could possibly want or desire. We are blessed!

I think if we would single out each and every blessing in our lives, we would see all the good that is there. We would feel honored to serve our spouse, our children, our family, our church, our purpose, our job, our home, our mind, our body, our possessions, etc. because we will know how valuable they truly are. Most importantly, when we single out God and focus on the ways He interacts with us, loves us, blesses us and forgives us; we would fall in love with Him anew each day.

"All praise to God, the Father of our Lord Jesus Christ, who has blessed us with every spiritual blessing in the heavenly realms because we are united with Christ. Even before he made the world, God loved us and chose us in Christ to be holy and without fault in his eyes" (Ephesians 1.3-4 NLT).

Rerouted to Favor

We went to Disney World Parks on our spring break. The kids were ecstatic when we finally crossed into the first park of our Disney adventure, Animal Kingdom. However, I was less than enthusiastic about the crowds and long lines. Never had I seen so many people converge in one place!

My husband got us Disney Fast Passes, but the Fast Pass to the main ride, Kilimanjaro Safaris, had run out. We were pretty disappointed because this ride allows the visitors to see the main animal attractions at the Animal Kingdom. The wait for the ride was 90 minutes, and the kids would not want to wait so long. We decided to skip the ride and enjoy the rest of the attractions that the park had to offer.

On our last Fast Pass ride, we went to one of the smaller rides at the park. The wait wasn't too long (25 minutes), so I tried to cheer myself up. We weren't getting to see the main attraction, but at least the kids were enjoying themselves. We finally made our way down the line, and we could see our seats coming around the corner. All of a sudden, a siren blared, and the Disney workers instantly escorted all of us back down the hall to the original entrance of the ride.

My oldest son was very upset. After waiting—what felt like to him to be an eternity—he never got to experience the ride. We calmed him down, and I explained that God always has a plan—even in our disappointments. As we left the entrance and walked into the sunlight, a worker was passing out slips of paper to every person leaving the ride. She gave one to each of the members of my family. I took mine and read it. It was a Fast Pass to any ride of our choice that day.

Then, I heard my husband say, "Let's go!" So we all scurried to follow him.

"Where are we going?" I asked, as I caught up.

"We are going to Kilimanjaro Safaris with our Fast Passes!" he declared.

We made it to the safari ride and presented our Fast Pass slip. The worker smiled and let us in. We hurried past the people waiting in the 90-minute line. I couldn't believe it! After a 10-minute walk, we were on our Safari jeep. My son quickly realized that what he thought had been a disappointment was actually his ticket to the best ride at the park!

By far, the Kilimanjaro Safaris ride was the highlight of our entire trip. We all learned a very important lesson. God sees the bigger picture, and He will detour us to get us on the right path to His best purposes for us. We must not grumble at the inconveniences along the way because they lead us on a better adventure with Him!

"And we know that in all things God works for the good of those who love him, who have been called according to his purpose" (Romans 8.28 NIV).

Carried Joy

My family and I were at an amazing water park on a hot day during summer break. It was one of those parks that had a multi-level fort with water shooting out of every nook and cranny. Sprays erupted from the ground like geysers, and water tumbled down in intricate waterfalls all around us. Kids and adults alike carried giant smiles, and laughter bubbled easily out of everyone's mouth. It was impossible not to have a good time in this wet extravaganza.

As I people-watched, I noticed a man running and playing in the water. His back was turned to me, but I could tell he was carrying a child. I thought it must have been a baby or a toddler at first, but I realized when he turned around that he was carrying a young boy around 10 or 11 years old. The boy's legs were paralyzed and his father became his support and strength.

The boy's joy-filled expression stole my attention, and I couldn't help but take part in his delight. He splashed the water with his hands as his father swung him through the cooling sprays. The father's expression was no less beautiful—it was clear that his satisfaction rested on his son's joy. They worked together in their play, and the cohesive bond they shared will always be a treasured memory tucked into the pocket of my soul.

As I rested in the sun watching the father and son duo, I felt the Holy Spirit tell me, "That's what I want with you."

God has such an amazing plan for each of us, but we will never achieve it on our own. Our human abilities are so limited compared to the awesome strength and power of our Heavenly Father, and it is only when we acknowledge our weaknesses that we will reach for His mercy and grace. God must carry us if we are to endeavor into our eternal purposes and enjoy the adventures that He has planned for us. However, we must put our complete dependence on Him.

God created us out of His overflowing love, and He died for us even in our imperfect state. He finds joy in caring for us, and He eagerly carries us further into His glory. We can trust Him completely and give our days over to His desire and design. And even in our shortcomings, we can rest assured that God loves us and yearns for us to find joy in His creation and company. If we would just partner up with His presence, the limits of this world would disappear under the weight of His sovereignty.

"But let the godly rejoice. Let them be glad in God's presence. Let them be filled with joy" (Psalm 68.3 NLT).

A Brisket Story

I sliced my thumb while cutting brisket.

My three kids were running around like crazed, hungry animals, and in my rush, I miscalculated the distance from the knife to my thumb. As I sliced, I knew I was about to be in a lot of pain. I was cutting hard because the brisket was lean. My wound was so deep that it had to be derma-glued together.

After about two weeks, the skin finally zipped up into a dandy little scar. Although my wound looked healed from the outside, I could tell that the inside was still tender. I would bump my thumb against a cupboard door while cooking or I would rub it across a hanger while doing laundry, and I would yelp in pain. Under normal circumstances, a thump or a rub wouldn't hurt my thumb; but since it had been injured, the smallest accidents would cause it to sting.

As I stared at my seemingly healed thumb, I contemplated how many times people feel intense pain from small offenses made by others. I know that in my life, I have struggled with the tenderness of serious wounds. Although they have healed, I still yelp out in pain when others accidentally bump or rub that injured area. The pain I feel doesn't match what occurred because I'm dealing with an issue that goes deeper into the ache of my heart.

I'm learning to analyze my feelings before I vent my anger toward a person who might have made a mistake or whose personality seems to aggravate my wound. I need to question whether I'm truly being mistreated or whether a tender area of the past is hurting. I strongly believe that my pain is a normal process of my healing, but I must realize that I need to give that pain to God. Only He will truly understand what I'm going through. I can give mercy to others and find my comfort in God.

"God blesses those who are merciful, for they will be shown mercy" (Matthew 5.7 NLT).

Odd Man Out

My oldest son is now in second grade. Having been homeschooled, he is the new kid in a class of students who have known each other since kindergarten, and he's having trouble finding someone to play with during recess. My husband and I have been giving him advice on how to make friends, and I've even contemplated asking the teacher to tell the students to include him in their play. Each day he'll come home with a hit or miss recess report. Sometimes he'll find a friend, but other times he just walks around and thinks.

Recently, when I was tucking him into bed, he told me, "Mommy, everyone has a two. I don't have my two."

"How many kids are in your class?" I asked.

"Seventeen," he replied.

"Oh, that's an odd number," I said.

"That's bad, isn't it, Mommy?" he whispered.

I told him that playing in a group of three is very fun, and he just needs to find a group of two to join, but in my mind I was thinking, "My son is the odd man out."

My husband and I started to worry about our son, but God encouraged us with the story of David before he became king. David was a shepherd boy and definitely the odd man out. He was alone most of the time, keeping company with only the sheep and his thoughts. However, God was able to cultivate a beautiful, intimate relationship with David during that time.

It is always nice when our kids are popular and included, but there is a reason when they are not. Right now my husband and I feel God leading us to allow our son to walk through this time of learning. Our son is beginning to feel the prompting of the Holy Spirit inside of him, and he's starting to take tiny steps of faith. We don't want to rob him of the spiritual growth God has planned for him.

It's hard to watch people we care about struggle, but we shouldn't always rescue them from being uncomfortable. God has a purpose behind every event in our life, especially the difficult ones; and we don't want to circumvent His movements because we don't like the process. God has an amazing purpose for my son, and He's already preparing him for the challenges along the way. I pray that God makes my son strong in faith, so he will make a difference for Christ.

"Yes, everything else is worthless when compared with the infinite value of knowing Christ Jesus my Lord. For his sake I have discarded everything else, counting it all as garbage, so that I could gain Christ" (Philippians 3.8 NLT).

Stop the Curse

I love the prophet Jeremiah. He found God's Word, devoured it and was forever changed. He talked about living for God, and how he became an outcast to the world for his faith. He prayed on behalf of God's chosen people, pleading for a nation that had forgotten their Creator.

As I was reading his dialogue with God, I was struck when God told him to stop praying (Jeremiah 14.11). I thought to myself, "Prayer must be a pretty powerful tool if God would command Jeremiah not to use it."

Earlier that day, I was reading a book by Derek Prince, and he wrote about how we can actually curse ourselves and others with our words. I made a connection between Jeremiah's powerful prayer to how powerful our curses can be. Our words have the power of life and death in them (Proverbs 18.21). I think we have grown so accustomed to speaking ugliness over ourselves and others that we don't even notice it. However, when we speak forth negative sentiments, are we not in fact offering up curses?

"I'm so fat. I'll never lose weight."

"She's going to ruin her life by marrying him."

"My son will never do well in school."

"My husband always says the wrong thing."

"That family will never break out of poverty."

Here's the thing. We might be speaking the physical truth as we see it, but God sees a potential that we can't understand when we are not looking through His eyes. In a split second, the circumstances we've labeled can change, and we are forever stuck with our ill-spoken words. Words are eternal and powerful, and we won't fully comprehend their potency until we are in heaven and surrounded by the words we spoke on earth.

My desire is to use my words to carve out godly, blessed lives for myself and others. If I could speak a beautiful truth over others again and again, maybe the path of righteousness will be easier for them to walk down. Maybe if I speak God's love over myself, I wouldn't struggle with carrying guilt, insecurity or hopelessness. Jesus died for each of us, and He looks beyond our faults and mistakes. I don't know about you, but I don't want to be caught speaking a curse that has the potential to harm one of God's children, including me! I think we simply need to speak God's truth more often and our "perceived" truth a lot less.

"But I tell you that everyone will have to give account on the day of judgment for every empty word they have spoken" (Matthew 12.36 NIV).

Losing God

I was putting my daughter into her car seat when she looked up at the moon, pointed and said, "Look, Mommy! The cow jumped over the moon!" I had to laugh a little because my two-year-old has no idea where that expression comes from or what it means. She heard it from her four-year-old brother, and he heard it from their seven-year-old brother. The expression was passed down from sibling to sibling, but the meaning was lost. The heart of any action, ideology and culture disappears when we don't take measures to explain it to the next generation.

The Old Testament Chosen People, the nation of Israel, were securely planted in the Promised Land because God loved them. They were not perfect, but God said that as long as they loved and obeyed Him and taught that devotion to their children, He would always be able to take care of them (Deuteronomy 6.3-9). The Chosen People could use their free will to stay under the protection of their Creator or to wander away from it. The choice of blessings or curses was ultimately theirs (Deuteronomy 30.19).

Flash forward several generations later and the people of Israel had forgotten about their One True God. God sent them prophet after prophet to remind His Chosen People about their covenant, but they wouldn't listen. As I was reading in Jeremiah about all the horrible effects of Israel's disobedience, I was struck by where God placed the guilt—He blamed the ancestors:

"When you tell these people all this and they ask you, 'Why has the LORD decreed such a great disaster against us? What wrong have we done? What sin have we committed against the LORD our God?' then say to them, 'It is because your ancestors forsook me,' declares the LORD, 'and followed other gods and served and worshiped them. They forsook me and did not keep my law. But you have behaved more wickedly than your ancestors. See how all of you are following the stubbornness of your evil hearts instead of obeying me'" (Jeremiah 16.10-12 NIV).

The ancestors forsook God and forgot to tell the next generation about how amazing our God is! Before the Chosen People knew it, their teachers had twisted the "word of the Lord" (Jeremiah 8.8), and they found themselves behaving even worse than their parents. There must have been a slow process of compromise in each generation for an entire nation to forget about their God; and if we are not careful, the New Testament Chosen People, Christians, will also find themselves outside of God's blessings!

Knowing God more is the purpose of life. Yes, we have responsibilities that keep us grounded in the world, but we can speak about God's love in our day-to-day activities. We have to make teaching those around us about God and having a relationship with Him through Jesus our first priority.

God blesses us every day, and we can share His goodness with others. We can't allow the things of this world to choke out His presence in our lives. We can change the fate of generations to come if we would only choose today not to compromise God's agenda for an easy, comfortable and self-centered life. When we find our purpose in God, we won't be able to keep quiet about all He is doing!

161

"But my life is worth nothing to me unless I use it for finishing the work assigned me by the Lord Jesus—the work of telling others the Good News about the wonderful grace of God" (Acts 20.24 NLT).

The Blue Noodle

I decided to take my seven, four and two-year-old to the pool at my gym. I filled the car with towels, swim toys and water noodles and prepared myself for an hour of aggressive mommy look-out time. One day I'll be able to accompany my children to the pool and let them play hog-wild by themselves in the water, but not today. I'm still in preschool stage, and there is no rest for this mom with tots—only a nice feeling of knowing my kids had fun.

After I parked, I got my kids out of the car and handed them each a towel, a swim toy and a water noodle. My oldest son got the green noodle, my middle son got the blue noodle and my little girl got the orange noodle. They looked absolutely adorable walking through the gym with their noodles sticking out of their hands like javelins. I weaved them through the workout machines and into the pool area. I loved hearing the comments like, "Your kids are so adorable." I nodded, smiled and thought to myself, "Yes, I know."

Once I got them to the pool, I took off their clothes and exposed their swimsuits like Superman in the phone booth, and we took to the stairs that led into the pool. The stairs are the only place in the pool that I can carefully monitor all three kids, so that is where we stayed for about an hour.

About halfway through our water-stair-fun, I noticed some other kids playing with a blue noodle. There were no other noodles in the entire pool besides the ones we brought, so I asked my four-year-old, "Is that your noodle?" He gave his best four-year-old answer: a shoulder shrug, which means I don't know. I made a mental note of the blue noodle and determined myself to get it before we left.

Finally, when it was time to go, I gathered all the noodles (including the blue one that I fetched when the culprits weren't looking), and we headed back through the gym. When we got to the car, I opened the rear door and was astonished to see a blue noodle inside.

My son had put the noodle back into the car before we left, and I had stolen a little boy's blue water noodle. When I examined the blue water noodles, I realized that they were totally different. Our noodle was brand-new, and the other one was old and torn. However, the evidence that I had gathered at the pool made it seem obvious to me that the other blue water noodle was mine. I unknowingly ignored all the minor details.

I felt God tell me, as I humbly returned the boy's water noodle, that everything is not always as it seems. Our eyes might make an assessment of certain situations, but God sees things that are beyond our comprehension. I believe that many times we force the wrong water noodles into our car, when God already has a brand-new water noodle waiting for us. I'm learning that I need to stop trying to understand and control everything; I need to humble myself; and I need wait patiently for God to reveal His blessings.

"But if we hope for something we do not yet see, we must learn how to wait for it" (Romans 8.25 NLV).

164

Receiving Mercy

I took my two sons (six-year-old and four-year-old) to an end of season soccer party. The kids got to play at a park, swim in a pool and jump on a trampoline. Many kids were running around having fun, but my oldest son was getting upset. One kid accidentally pushed him on the trampoline. Another kid unknowingly hit his eye with a water noodle. And a girl on a swing ran into him while he was walking through the playground.

My son cried to me, "Why do kids keeping hurting me?"

"They are not doing it on purpose," I told him in my sweetest mommy voice. "There are a lot of kids here, so they're going to bump into each other."

"But, they are hitting me, and I don't like it!" He screamed.

"Well, the only thing we can do is make all the kids go home, so you can play by yourself. Does that sound fun to you?" I asked him.

"No," he answered.

"You have to understand that people accidentally hurt each other, so you have to give them mercy. No one is perfect, and we all make mistakes."

"Okay, Mommy," he said and went back into the pool.

Ten minutes later, I found my son standing with his head buried in a lawn chair. He looked like an ostrich hiding his face in the sand.

"What happened," I asked him.

He looked at me. His eyes were red and swollen, and his cheeks were wet with tears.

"I accidentally pushed a girl!" he whispered.

"How?" I asked

"I was on the trampoline, and I ran into her!" he said, getting louder.

"Did you say sorry?" I asked.

"Yes," he said, "but everyone looked at me!"

"It's okay," I said pointing to the trampoline. "Look, they are all jumping again. They don't even remember."

"But, I ran into her, and they all looked at me!" he yelled.

I knew my son needed additional insight on mercy. "Guess what, Son? You are not perfect either. You also make mistakes, and you will need to receive mercy from others."

"But I hurt her!" he screamed with fresh tears falling down his face.

I took my son into my arms and gave him a big hug. "I think you also need to give yourself a little mercy too."

As I held my son, I realized that I also struggle with giving myself mercy. Through the years, I've learned to give mercy to others, but I never quite got the knack of receiving it. I'm hard on myself, and I tend to focus on my mistakes. I don't give myself any slack, and this makes my life tense when I'm in a particularity difficult season.

I know that there is a balance between grace and diligence, and I'm determined to figure it out. I don't want to limit God when I try to stick myself into a mold of perfection. I will never be perfect, and I will hurt and offend people, but I trust that God will transform my mistakes into something beautiful. I want to lean on His perfection and allow His grace to fill in the cracks of my imperfection. Hopefully, my son and I can step into the fullness of His mercy together.

"But for that very reason I was shown mercy so that in me, the worst of sinners, Christ Jesus might display his immense patience as an example for those who would believe in him and receive eternal life" (1 Timothy 1.16 NIV).

Faith Journey

My son is learning to type using a computer program. Today was his third day, and he was slowly typing the middle row of keys, trying not to look at his fingers. There were about eight lines showing; and as he typed each line, another line would appear on the bottom. After five minutes of typing, he finally looked at me.

"New lines keep coming up, Mommy. When is this going to end?" he asked anxiously.

I said, "Type a few more lines, and you'll probably see the end come up soon."

He went back to typing, but it was obvious by the way he was slouching in his chair and by the irritable expression on his face that he had lost hope of ever seeing the end to his lesson.

Suddenly, he punched the last key on the line he was typing, and the final sentence came into sight. He was about four lines away from finishing. My son's back straightened and a smile spread across his face. He was almost there!

It's interesting how a good dose of perspective can help you see something through to the end.

Many times in my Christian journey, I've had to walk out on faith. Sometimes my acts of faith are immediately confirmed; other times, however, I'm a million steps into "Faith-land" without any physical signs that I'm going the right way.

I feel God's Spirit in me approving my direction, but it would be so nice if I could see the Promised Land on the other end! Often, I become disillusioned, and I feel like giving up and not finishing. But God graciously renews my strength right when I need it most. There are some faith-journeys that I'm on that God is in the double digits of giving me a strength-renewal!

Though the ending may not be in sight, I know that God works all things for His good. I know that He loves me, and He wants the best for me. And I know that He would rescue me and redirect my steps if I somehow lost my way.

By faith I choose to straighten my back and put a smile on my face because I know that I'm offering my life to the purposes of my Creator, and He will not steer me wrong. I trust that He has amazing plans for me, and I believe His Word and the promptings of the Holy Spirit.

"Blessed are those whose strength is in you, whose hearts are set on pilgrimage" (Psalm 84.5 NIV).

The Christmas Photo

My kids were all ready for pictures with Santa. My sons wore cute red and green plaid shirts, red sweater vests and corridor pants, and my daughter wore a beautiful Christmas dress that I bought last spring on clearance. I couldn't wait to grace the entrance of the mall and present my picturesque kids to Santa and the photo elves. Wouldn't they all just swoon over my angelic children?

Amazingly enough, my sons both smiled and waited patiently for the camera to flash. My daughter, on the other hand, took one look at the stranger wearing a red suit and donning a long white beard and freaked out. My husband and I tried our best to get her to smile, and the photo elves took several shots, but my daughter's screams only grew louder and her tears only grew fatter. She reached her little arms toward me and called out "Mama!" Never once did she look in the direction of the camera.

In Christmases past, I would have been irritated about the wasted energy and the less than perfect Christmas photo, and I would have allowed my disappointment to steal a little of my Christmas joy. However, this year was different. I felt a tinge of frustration, but it was quickly overpowered by my enjoyment in the honest reaction of my child. I held my daughter in my arms and praised her instincts: "I'm so proud of you! You distrust strangers and that is a very good thing!"

As I walked with my husband back through the mall to let our kids play on the soft park, I thought about what had changed in me. Since I've only been a mother for six years, I prayed that God would help me understand the good work He had performed in me. I came to the conclusion that our children are not here to meet our expectations or to fulfill our happiness; rather, they are here to live out the purposes of God.

I believe that having standards for our children is good; but when we start pushing them to meet our expectations, or worse yet, other people's expectations that we fear, we have placed a large burden on their shoulders that they were never meant to carry. As parents, we are called to obediently follow God's lead in caring for our children (allowing His grace to fill the holes of our mistakes), and God will take care of the rest. It is HIS job to fulfill the purposes that He has for them.

After I finally digested this truth, I realized that I would have less disappointments, frustrations and irritation if I didn't drive myself and everyone around me to meet MY expectations. Only God knows the future, and He is the only One who has perfect expectations. When I relinquish my desires for His, I can live my life in peace, joy and hope no matter what is going on around me. This year's Christmas photo will always bring a smile to my face, because I know that even my daughter's cries have fulfilled the purposes of God.

"And we know that in all things God works for the good of those who love him, who have been called according to his purpose" (Romans 8.28 NIV).

The Gift of Contentment

We were at the beach, and my oldest son was collecting seashells. I asked him what he was going to do with all of them. He said he was going to make a necklace for a special girl. I thought of all the little girls in his circle of friends, and one in particular came to mind. I asked, "Does her name start with a C?"

He said, "No, her name starts with an L."

I went through the short list of little girl L names I knew, even mentioning some of the mommies with L names. But with a smile, he said no to each one. Then I thought of my name. Although my name is Alisa (uh-lĭs-uh), my husband usually takes out the beginning A and calls me (lĭs-uh).

I called my son close to me and whispered in his ear, "Is it lĭsa?" He smiled and blushed and nodded his head yes. I gave him a big hug, and all that day I felt like a treasure. My son may have confused my name, but it didn't affect how I felt about his eagerness to bless me.

Isn't it beautiful how the love we have will overlook the small mistakes and focus on the show of devotion? However, when I thought about this, I remembered that early in my marriage I was not very good at forgiving oversights. My husband would go out of his way to do something nice, but many times it wasn't according to my anticipation. I would zero in on what I didn't like, instead of appreciating the beauty of his sacrifice.

After a time, my husband stopped trying to do special things to spoil me. I didn't blame him, because I had filled his gift-offerings with negative energy. Why would he continue giving when he could never get it right? I quickly discovered my mistake and worked hard to reverse the damage I created. I changed my perspective and openly accepted everything he did for me and gave me. Moreover, I started to realize that I enjoyed his taste and ideas. Now my husband rocks at giving!

We live in a very self-indulged society. We are used to getting everything exactly how we want it; and if we don't, we show our discontent. We are swimming in blessings, and we don't realize that everything we receive is a gift. When we start being picky, we might need to shed off some pounds of selfishness and let go of our self-entitled attitude. The gift is not as important as the person who gives it.

"I am not saying this because I am in need, for I have learned to be content whatever the circumstances" (Philippians 4.11 NIV).

Stand Your Ground

My son loves to chase birds. When he sees them sweetly sitting there, he takes off into a sprint toward them. The birds instantly fly away as they see my son heading like a freight train in their direction. He divides the birds like the red sea, and he grins with a feeling of triumph.

One afternoon, I took my kids to the splash park. A single bird sat in the water enjoying herself immensely. My son ran toward her, but the bird didn't budge; she didn't even ruffle a feather. Her fearlessness caused my son to abruptly stop. The bird stood her ground, and my son walked away. I figured my son only enjoyed the chase-and-run game when the birds cooperated.

God has been teaching me a lot about standing my ground. Many times I'm others-centered instead of God-centered, and I worry way too much what people think. If I have to make a decision that others don't like, I show my fear, guilt and apprehension of their opinion concerning my decision. Unknowingly, others take this as a cue that I'm in the wrong and that their disapproval of my decision is justified.

I try to root all of my decisions in God, and, honestly, many people don't like my choices. When I show my angst about my decision,

I'm indicating that I approve of other people's disapproval, and I reveal a lack of trust in God's judgment. The impression I give is not fair to others or to me because it causes a bunch of negative undertones that wouldn't be there if I were to simply take my insecurity out of my decision making.

I'm learning to be like that bird and stand my ground. Others see my sincerity (even if they don't agree), and they back away. Plus, I'm not conflicted with emotional stress that my uncertainty causes. If God is the core of all that I do, I don't have to worry about the waves that my life creates.

When Jesus lived, many people disagreed and misunderstood Him. But no one could doubt His sincerity. He never worried about what others thought because He was only concerned with what God thought. I want to be like Jesus. Even in the middle of complete chaos, I desire to be assured and confident with my God-aligned choices.

"Be on your guard; stand firm in the faith; be courageous; be strong" (1 Corinthians 16.13 NIV).

Where's the Sugar

I made a sugar free apple cobbler for my kids. Even the whipped cream on top was sugar free. I was so excited because it looked beautiful, and it tasted pretty good. My three-year-old sugar connoisseur son was so excited. I put the dessert in front of him, and his eyes bulged. He took his spoon and started taking big bites. After a few mouthfuls, he put the spoon down and looked up at me.

"What's wrong?" I said. "You don't like it?"

He pushed the bowl away and said, "It needs sugar."

I couldn't believe it. I looked at my husband, and he shrugged. How did he know there was no sugar?

The same concept can be applied to ministry. A ministry leader can make sure that everything is perfect and looks great, but there is only one way to ensure that God's sweetness (Holy Spirit) is present. Unless the leadership is sensitive and broken to the will of God, the Holy Spirit cannot freely move through the ministry like it should.

Before we had kids, God moved my husband and me to Dallas. I saw a commercial for a local Christian school, and I knew that God wanted me to teach there. The position paid very little, so I taught college at night. The year was challenging for me, and I couldn't wait until summer so I could get outside the classroom.

I started applying to other positions, but I had an uneasy feeling that I was supposed to teach one more year. I got offered an amazing job located in downtown Dallas, creating English software to help kids with standardized testing. I was ecstatic because this job paid twice the amount of my two current positions combined, and I could sit behind a computer and analyze grammar and syntax all day.

For five days, I wrestled with God. I knew He didn't want me to take the job. I remember jogging on my treadmill, and I jumped so hard out of anger that I broke it. I stomped around my living room and finally fell against the wall crying. I cried until there was nothing left. My family and friends didn't understand. Why would I not go for such an amazing opportunity? All I could say was, "God says so."

During the last day of school, I finally resolved to be obedient, but I still felt very abandoned by God. I went to my desk and opened the Bible. I read Jeremiah 29.11: "'For I know the plans I have for you,' says the LORD. 'They are plans for good and not for disaster, to give you a future and a hope'" (NLT). I decided that I would learn everything God wanted to teach me the following year, so, hopefully, He would allow me to leave the classroom.

My last year teaching, I taught seven subjects, including seventh and eighth grade Physical Education. For one of the six weeks, I felt God wanted me to teach them a Christian song in sign language. I didn't know anything about music, but two of my students were daughters of the choir teacher. I didn't have a plan, so we just worked each day at putting together a performance. I taught the girls some "choreography" and the sisters helped with the chorus. We finally finished it, and the girls had created something special.

I saw the principal in the hall, and I asked if she wouldn't mind just taking a quick look at what the girls had created. She said sure, and sat down in an empty auditorium. After the principal saw it, she demanded that they perform in front of the school at the next pep rally. The girls were thrilled, and I was happy that they were able to show the school how hard they worked.

The girls performed in front of the entire school, and the teachers and students were amazed. People were crying, and I didn't understand what was going on. The choir director came up to me with tears in her eyes and said, "Now that's what it's all about." Until this day I value the fact that she didn't thank me. It was obvious that I did nothing except allow myself to be broken by God and stay obedient to His will.

God's Spirit is unleashed through the brokenness of the ministry leader. Leaders are called into dry areas, so Living Water can flow through them, saturating everything with God's presence. However, the ministry leaders must be broken so that the Holy Spirit in them can move freely. Leaders are responsible for having a broken self-nature and an obedient heart; the rest is up to God.

God's glory comes in all shapes and forms and through all types of ministries, but it is obvious when the Holy Spirit is present....you can taste His sweetness. God needs our brokenness, so the Holy Spirit in us has free reign.

"Our bodies are buried in brokenness, but they will be raised in glory. They are buried in weakness, but they will be raised in strength. They are buried as natural human bodies, but they will be raised as spiritual bodies. For just as there are natural bodies, there are also spiritual bodies" (1 Corinthians 15.43-44 NLT).

A Good Fear

My oldest son has taken swim lessons since he was six months old. Every summer we pour energy, money and time into getting him acquainted with the water and comfortable swimming. By the end of each summer, he is able to confidently move through the water like a fish!

However, through the winter months, his water skills take a back seat and he loses his swimming confidence. When summer comes around again, he believes he can't swim and is burdened by an unfounded fear.

Once again, I enrolled my son in swim lessons, and the teacher assessed him in the water. He was nervous and wouldn't let go of the side. She said that he would have to go with the beginners who were several years younger than he.

I was discouraged because I knew he could do better. I saw his fear and tried to explain to him that he was an amazing swimmer—he had just forgotten! He wouldn't listen to me, though. His fear dictated his actions and drove his mother crazy!

During the first swim lesson, my son regained his confidence; and by the second swim lesson, the teacher had to move him to the next class. He was far more advanced than she had anticipated. When he finally let go of his fear, he was able to demonstrate his real ability.

And don't we do that too as God's children?

God is constantly working in us to prepare us for the challenges ahead. He knows who we are deep in our spirits, and He knows that we can do His will. But many times our fears stop us from shining His glory. I can go through all the reasons and excuses of our fears, but I'll just touch on the deepest root: We have lost our fear (reverence, honor, awe) of God, and that fear has been transmitted to the world.

If the Creator of life, the God of everything living, and the King of all that breathes says that we can do it, what right do we have to yell back, "No, we can't"? Are we going to bow down to the fear of God or the fear of the world?

If God says you can do it—YOU CAN!

I want to be an excellent wife—YOU CAN!

I want to raise godly children—YOU CAN!

I want to serve with a heart of joy—YOU CAN!

I want to accomplish the impossible—YOU CAN!

I want to be a shining woman of faith—YOU CAN!

You can swim in this crazy ocean of faith. God has given you the tools, and He is slowly honing your talent during the seemingly meaningless tasks that you do every day. He is doing a good work in you. He knows when you are ready to swim, so when you hear Him calling you out, don't think about it, don't analyze it, don't worry about it and don't fret about it. Just tell yourself, "I can!"

If you have submitted to His authority and have been faithful in the small things of your daily life, you will find victory. And when you finally start swimming, you'll realize that you had more ability than you anticipated. God will have to pile on more anointing just to keep up with your skills. Take off the weight of fear, and you'll rise to the top!

"I can do all this through him who gives me strength" (Philippians 4.13 NIV).

Just Five Pounds

I had been avoiding the scale for several weeks, but I finally decided to weigh myself and account for the damage. Yep, I had gained five pounds. My weight always fluctuates. I think it enjoys making me mad, happy or sad based on its movements; it likes to show off its control over me.

Normally when I gain weight, I focus all my attention and efforts on the unwanted pounds. I lose all my peace and joy, and every aspect of my daily life is affected. I'm determined to lose the weight at all cost.

As my mind started its downward spiral of negative and distracting thoughts, God told me, "They don't make a difference."

"What?" I asked. I was really tired of this cycle, and I was willing to hear what God had to say.

"Those five pounds you are worrying about make absolutely no difference in your life. They don't affect how people see you, they don't affect your health and they don't affect your destiny. They are meaningless."

After God gave me the truth about my five pounds, I finally found freedom. I didn't want to waste my energy over a few pounds because I'm busy enough doing things that have purpose. Why would I misuse my time on something that is insignificant? I felt light as a feather, though I was five pounds heavier!

In my newfound freedom, I got dressed. I didn't even worry about the fact that my jeans were a tad snugger around my waist. Since my mind was freed up to think about more important things, I started focusing on God's promises for me. My thoughts instantly started exploring what I needed to do in order for God to finally fulfill His plans for my life.

God said almost cheekily, "They don't make a difference."

"What?" I asked. If God had more freedom for me, I wanted it.

During my entire adult life, I have struggled with trying to humble myself more, trying to learn more, trying to shed more sin, trying to focus on God more. I've wanted to do everything in my power, so I could prove to God that I was ready to receive His promises. Without knowing it, though, I was basing God's promises on what I was doing.

God said, "Nothing you could ever do would make you deserve the promises that I have for you. My promises will always be too great for you to earn. I give them freely to you because of who I am and because I love you."

Talk about freedom! All my efforts could never secure God's blessings, so I can quit worrying about proving myself all the time. God blesses me because of what He has done, not what I have done. All I need to do is focus on staying in God's will. If I am in the center of His purpose, God will accomplish His plans for me. I simply need to cooperate with Him.

I also realized that God gives all of us five pounds of grace. When you look at an imperfect woman and wonder why she's getting blessed, just remember that she has five pounds of grace. And the same goes for you. If you see your imperfections and wonder how God could ever bless you, just remember that God has five pounds of grace for you too. All of us make mistakes.

None of us deserve God's blessing. I don't care how perfect you are or how perfect you think she is. Our efforts are meaningless compared to God's perfection. We all deserve death if it wasn't for Christ!

Christians can claim God's grace, and that is why we can boldly go to the throne! God has an amazing life for us, and He gives it to us freely. We just have to be available and willing to receive it. Finally, five pounds we can all rejoice about!

"For it is by grace you have been saved, through faith-and this not from yourselves, it is the gift of God—not by works, so that no one can boast" (Ephesians 2.8-9 NIV).

The Kneeling Circle

For several days, a certain spiritual leader kept coming to my mind. My thoughts would sporadically center on this person, so I decided to pray for him, hoping my mind would be able to refocus once I said, "amen." As I prayed, however, I couldn't shake the feeling that I was missing something.

One day, I opened up a devotional book that I read to my children every morning. This book is a collection of real life faith stories by children all around the world. This day's devotional was about a girl that woke up in the middle of the night thinking about her brother. The girl became restless with thoughts of her brother, so she decided to pray for him.

From about 12am – 4am she prayed for her brother who was at church camp, and the Holy Spirit guided her in the exact words He wanted her to say. She finally drifted off to sleep and was awoken several hours later by the concerned voice of her mother. A camp counselor had found a tick on her brother's scalp. The tick was a carrier of the Rocky Mountain Spotted Fever disease. The brother was rushed to the hospital, and the doctors were able to remove the tick and take care of the sickness before it became fatal.

After I read this story to my children, the spiritual leader I had been praying for came to my mind again. I felt the Holy Spirit say, "Now I want you to REALLY pray for him."

I suddenly stopped in the middle of the kitchen and told my three kids that I was going to kneel to pray. I knelt and bowed my head, allowing the Holy Spirit to feed me the words that He wanted me to say. I can't remember exactly what I prayed, but I know my words had meaning and purpose.

When I finished my prayer, I opened my eyes to a small circle of kneeling kids around me. I heard my two boys and little girl say, "amen," and they looked up at me with precious, smiling expressions. At that moment, God gave me a deeper understanding of prayer, and He also blessed me with a beautiful image of my kids kneeling in a circle—a memory I will never forget.

"For where two or three gather in my name, there am I with them" (Matthew 18.20 NIV).

A Blue Shirt Prayer

Since summer is coming into full swing, I decided to wear a beachy outfit to church. *I do live in a coastal town*, I thought. I pulled on a jean skirt that hit just above my knees and slipped on a pair of flip-flops. Then, I stood in front of the row of colorful shirts lining my closet. *What would be the perfect leisure shirt to wear?* I wondered.

My eyes traveled past the button-up collared shirt–too formal; beyond the embroidered t-shirt–too simple; and over the stretchy black and white shirt—to monochromatic. Finally, I beheld a white, cotton polo style shirt that I had just purchased—too perfect!

However, before I took the shirt off of the hanger, I felt the Holy Spirit whisper, "What about the blue one?"

When I find a shirt that I really like, I sometimes buy two of them in different colors. This way I can enjoy the same style shirt more frequently. I remembered that when I bought the white shirt, I also bought a blue one.

Okay, I figured. It doesn't really make a difference which color I wear. Denim goes with everything! I searched through my closet quickly, knowing that I had only a few minutes to finish getting ready. I gave one last sweep with my eyes before giving up the search when I finally spied the blue shirt squished between two other garments.

I swiftly tugged the shirt off the hanger, yanked it over my head and hurried back to the bathroom mirror to finish putting on my makeup. As my family and I headed off to get tacos before church, I forgot all about my shirt swop. The Holy Spirit leads me in little, crazy ways; and I have long since given up questioning His direction.

When tacos were consumed, we leisurely walked to the car. My older two boys can buckle their own seatbelts, but my husband and I take turns buckling up our four-year-old girl. Since it was my husband's turn to do the honors, I waited in the front seat, watching the people walk by. Suddenly, I noticed a woman wearing a blue cotton polo style shirt, heading toward the restaurant. I looked at the emblem on the shirt and realized it was the exact shirt that I was wearing!

"Pray for her," the Holy Spirit whispered.

I don't believe in coincidences. I know for a fact that God orchestrated my morning, so I could notice that woman. I prayed for her every day until the Holy Spirit lifted the burden. I had no clue what I was praying for, but the Holy Spirit knew what she needed (Romans 8.26). I used my free will to speak God's truth into another person's life, and not for one second do I believe my words came back void.

"Pray in the Spirit at all times and on every occasion. Stay alert and be persistent in your prayers for all believers everywhere" (Ephesians 6.18 NLT).

Taste God's Good

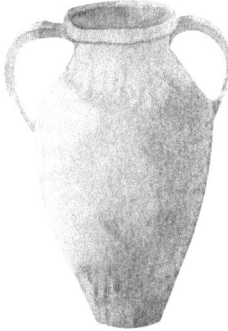

My daughter is now fifteen months old, and it seems that the third child grows way too quickly. She now says several words. One of her favorite words to say is "food." Whatever I give her—oatmeal, a sandwich, chicken or a cookie—she calls it food.

I wanted to start distinguishing each food item, but I could tell that the advancement in communication would be too much for her. She just caught onto what "food" meant, and I wouldn't want to confuse her. Food is the stuff that she puts in her mouth when her tummy rumbles. That's all she needed to know at the moment.

While watching my daughter eat, I thought of the verse, "Taste and see that the LORD is good" (Psalm 34.8a NIV). There are so many good qualities of God, and many times I never bother to distinguish them. I just call every aspect of His awesome character "good." However, I do want to start recognizing the many qualities of His divine nature. I want to understand the taste of each blessing.

If God forgives me for a wrong that I continually commit, I want to claim His mercy. If God reveals something beautiful through me, I want to claim His glory. If God does the impossible in my life, I want to claim His grace. And if God redeems a wrong that has been forced on me, I want to claim His justice.

God does so many good things for me and through me every day, and I want to passionately point out each one and name it. I think if I can start recognizing the essence of His goodness, I will learn more about how amazing our God is. I want to taste each blessing and savor each flavor.

"Like newborn babies, crave pure spiritual milk, so that by it you may grow up in your salvation, now that you have tasted that the Lord is good" (1 Peter 2.2-3 NIV).

Uncomfortable Faith

Our family dog, Rusty, hates driving in cars. His miniature dachshund body quivers, and he whimpers nervous cries. He anxiously jumps up and down on the car seats, so the kids have learned to hold him securely. When he looks out of the car window, he whines impatiently, and it's obvious to all of us that he can't wait until the car ride is over.

But the interesting thing is that when we head toward the hallway that leads to the garage, he automatically runs with us. Most of the time, we leave him in the house when we go into town, and we always wind up carrying him back into the house. He scrambles to jump into the car when we open the door, trying to make it in before we can catch him.

As I carried him back into the house one particular morning—after not shutting the door leading into the garage quick enough to stop Rusty's mad dash to the car—I wondered why he was so desperate to go with us. There was no mistaking that he greatly disliked our car rides, but somehow he still willingly made his way toward the garage every time we tried to leave.

And I felt the Holy Spirit say, "He loves his family more than He dislikes car rides."

Rusty would rather be with us in the dreaded car than be home alone without us, and that is so much like our relationship with God. God leads us into situations that are uncomfortable because He knows they will break and grow us. But many times, we avoid stepping out in obedience because we allow fear to cause us to disobey His will.

However, our love for God should greatly outweigh our dislike of the situation. If God's presence is leading us onto an uncomfortable path, circumstance or choice, we need to trust that His will is perfect. And even if we don't want to go, we have to be willing to say, "I'd rather be with God in the eye of the storm than be safe on the shore without Him."

"Overhearing what they said, Jesus told him, 'Don't be afraid; just believe'" (Mark 5.36 NIV).

Two Beaches

I had a few minutes to spare while the kids were at VBS (Vacation Bible School), so I headed to the beach for a quick run on the sand.

There are two stretches of beach lining the coast where I live. Before the pier, the sand is populated with vacationers and beach dwellers. As I ran, I had to carefully watch where I was going. I didn't want to charge into a kid building sandcastles or smash into a man grilling hot dogs.

I ran barefoot, so I had to stay aware of where I placed my feet. There were bottle caps, broken glass and other manmade objects littering the beach. The run on this side of the beach caused me to stay focused on my surroundings and the people around me.

Once I passed the pier, however, I felt like I had instantly entered into my own uncharted oasis. This beach was free of people and debris. Large pelicans rested on the beach. I could run without looking down, and every time I stepped, I felt the soft sand under my feet.

No noise, no litter, no distraction. As I ran, I focused on God and the beauty of His creation. I almost wanted to never run on the other beach again, but I realized that I had parked my car over on the other side. I had to go through chaos to get to the peace of God.

God will do just that in our spiritual lives. He will "park" some area of our lives in the center of human interaction. Whether it be our family, career, ministry, etc., we are called to be the hands and feet of Jesus to this world. We cannot stay isolated in our own uncharted oasis all the time.

Just like Jesus, though, we can slip away when the noise of this world gets too much and seek solace with God; but once we are rested and refreshed, God will send us out into the world to show His love to His children. We can be attentive to when the Holy Spirit is leading us into His work or into His rest.

"But Jesus Himself would often slip away to the wilderness and pray" (Luke 5.16 NASB).

The Beach

My family lives close to the Gulf of Mexico, so one day after church, we decided to head to the beach. We hadn't been in a while—the summer weeks have been racing past us—and our kids have been asking daily to go. We finally relented. We reached the beach. I sprayed the kids down with sunblock, and they ran straight to the warm waves.

I loved watching them smile and laugh as they splashed through the salty current. It was a perfect day—blue skies, slight breeze and smooth ripples. I couldn't help but thank God for our Texas coast and promise myself that I would not neglect this beautiful blessing from God. Suddenly, I saw my husband gesturing to the water. I walked closer to his location, and I could hear the wind carry his voice with the words: "Portuguese Man O' War."

I called my kids to me and walked them back to the sandy shore. Then we passed the dangerous water creature's location and went back into the water. My kids asked me what was going on, so I let them know that there was a Portuguese Man O' War in the water, and we were simply going around it.

I could tell that the kids were frightened, so I gently told them about the realities of the beach. The water is wonderful and it is a blessing, but there are also dangers in it that we need to be careful of. But we can't let the possibility of danger prevent us from enjoying God's vast waters. Fear should not rule our actions.

This reality is true for life, as well. As we go about our day, there will always be potential for dangers, but we can't be ruled by fear. We must live in an atmosphere of faith. Yes, we may get hurt, but God is with us every step of the way. Jesus died for our sins, so He could live every moment of life—the good and the bad—with us. He will never leave us nor forsake us, so we don't need to live in fear.

And one day, we won't ever feel pain or heartache again. Because of Jesus' sacrifice on the cross, heaven is available to everyone who receives Him as their Lord and Savior.

"The LORD himself goes before you and will be with you; he will never leave you nor forsake you. Do not be afraid; do not be discouraged" (Deuteronomy 31.8 NIV).

Faith Words of the Imagination

A Mother's Fight on the Mountain

The Mother stood firmly on the base of the mountain. She anchored herself to her sword, alert to the Enemy's arrows of condemnation flying all around her. One of the arrows pierced her thigh, but she no longer cried out. Half a dozen arrows had already dug into her flesh, and the stings combined to form a continual ache. She gripped her shield, determined not to let another arrow find its mark.

Other soldiers walked past her to make their way up the mountain. She envied their freedom to climb, and her eyes traveled their direction to the mountaintop. She could see God's glory radiating at the pinnacle, but she quickly turned away when an arrow zipped past her cheek.

A seasoned soldier stopped to look at her.

"I see that you are a strong warrior and that you fight with dignity. I'm leading these new soldiers to the top. Why don't you join us? You are more than ready," the soldier said.

"I cannot leave my post," the Mother said. "I have been called to protect the base of the mountain."

"But you are no longer a new Christian. In fact, it is obvious that you have already surpassed many levels of the mountain. Why do you stay here at the bottom when you can easily make it to the top?" he pushed further.

The Mother looked away from the soldier and secured herself more tightly to her sword. "I have been called to stay here," she said, resolutely. "I don't know why, but I must obey."

"But you haven't even used your sword," the soldier countered.

"I may not be wielding my sword like you, but I am using it. It keeps me grounded to my position," the Mother said.

The soldier wanted to say more, but the Mother turned her attention back to the battle line. He gripped his sword, adjusted his shield and continued his climb to the next level.

A time later, a young woman entered through the base of the mountain and stood next to the Mother, setting her shield on the ground. "Can you help me?" she asked. "I can't keep up with the others, and I don't know how to get to the top alone."

The Mother looked at the young woman, holding her shield up further to protect them both. "I cannot go with you, but I can tell you what I have learned. It will help you reach the next level."

The young woman thought for a moment. "I wish you would take me, but I'm sure your words will prove useful."

The Mother reached in her pocket and handed a journal to the young woman. "Here is all I know. Take it with you, and you will find understanding as you travel farther."

"But I don't want to take all your words," the young woman protested.

"Do not worry," the Mother encouraged. "Every time I reach into this pocket, a new journal appears. I have given out many to other young soldiers like you."

The young woman smiled and opened the book. The Mother continued to block the arrows as she read. The words brightened the young woman's face.

"I can tell from your words that you have already made it to the top of the mountain," the young woman said.

The Mother's eyes gazed at the top where God's glory shined. "I haven't seen the top with my eyes, but my heart has been there many times."

"But how could you write about the top with such detail if you haven't been there? How do you know the path to take if you've never walked it?" the young woman asked confused.

"I have walked it many times by faith," the Mother replied. "Since I'm not allowed to leave the base of the mountain, I must use the eyes of my heart and the spirit of belief to visit the top."

"Are you sure you don't want to go with me and experience the top for yourself?" the young woman asked.

"No," the Mother said and drove her sword deeper into the soil. "I have been called to protect the base."

The young woman stared at the Mother for a moment. "Well, thank you for the words," she finally said. She put the journal into her pocket, picked up her shield and started her climb to the next level.

Finally, the sky darkened, and the Mother sat down to rest. The arrows halted their flight for a time, but the Mother kept her shield against her body as a precaution. She pulled the sword out from the ground, and it morphed into a small pen. She took out the journal from her pocket and began to write—every now and then she would look at the mountaintop and whisper soft prayers.

As she prayed, she saw a light descending down the side of the mountain. The light became brighter as seconds went by, and suddenly it filled the base of the mountain where she sat. A man stood in front of her with books filling his arms, and the light from the mountaintop reflected off his gold armor. He unloaded his burden next to the Mother and sat on the ground beside her shield.

"Do you want to sit behind my shield," the Mother offered, squinting her eyes from the bright reflection of the light.

"No, the arrows no longer pierce me," he said with a smile.

"You have been to the top of the mountain," the Mother stated.

"Yes, I have," he said with a nod.

"Is that why your armor shines?" she asked.

"Yes, but only for a time. I will travel to many levels of this mountain, and the dirt and grime will subdue the glow," he answered.

"Will you be sad?" the Mother asked.

"No, people are more willing to take my words when they are not blinded," he said. "Besides, I can go back to the top anytime and my armor will be like new again."

"What's it like at the top?" the Mother asked.

"It's the most amazing place I have ever seen," he answered.

The Mother looked up. "I wish I could go up there."

"You have," he said.

The Mother looked at the man. "I know I've been there by faith, but I long to really experience it," she said.

"You will," he said. "But now you are needed here."

"I know," she said, looking down at her journal. "I must be patient."

"What you are doing here is very important," the man said.

"I don't feel like I do much," the Mother said honestly. "I share my words with those who are seeking, but other than that, I only protect the base of the mountain."

The man looked at her surprised. "You are not protecting the mountain," he said.

The Mother looked at the man's eyes. The light from his face began to warm her cold skin. "What do you mean?"

"You are protecting them," he said, pointing to her lap. She looked down and saw her three children curled up safely against her. Her two younger children were asleep, and the oldest looked up at her intently.

"I no longer feel the weight of them," the Mother said, staring tenderly at her young children. "Their burden is my joy."

"They are the reason you must wait," he said softly.

The Mother stroked the cheeks of her two sleeping children and nodded at her oldest with a smile. "I would do anything for them," she said in a hushed voice.

The man nodded his approval. "You have taken their arrows and kept them safe from the attacks of the Enemy. The two that are sleeping haven't been awakened to salvation yet, but they soon will be. And you see the oldest? He is watching you, learning from your every move. When he is ready, he will move quickly up this mountain and bring many soldiers with him."

The Mother put down her pen, so she could wipe the tears with the back of her hand. "I didn't realize," she managed.

The man began to gently pull out each arrow from the woman's flesh. "You are very strong because you have learned to be patient and to obey. Your journey may seem slow, and it may be difficult to see others pass you by; but you carry a heavy load. Your children will be great warriors at a very young age because of your obedience. They will change the world for Christ."

The woman thought of the many years she waited without knowing why. "Your words have renewed my hope," she said.

"The Master has sent me to encourage you," the man replied. "He wants me to tell you that He is pleased with your belief."

"My belief?" the Mother asked not fully understanding.

"Your belief helps you to abide in the mountaintop that He placed inside your heart," he said, pointing to her. "That mountain is where God's presence dwells."

The Mother laid her hand on her chest and closed her eyes, as the revelation began to take root.

"I must go," the man said, getting up.

"I understand," the Mother said, looking back up at him. "Thank you for sharing your words with me."

"I brought more of my words," he said, motioning to the stack of books. "Read them and stay rooted in His Word, and you will gain peace and courage to stand strong."

The Mother took one of the books and flipped through its pages. "Yes, I already feel strengthened," she confirmed.

"I am glad. It gives me joy in my sacrifice," he said and turned to leave.

"Wait!" the Mother called out. "I'll see you at the top someday."

The man smiled. "Sooner than you think," he said and disappeared.

Flying with Jesus

The woman saw Jesus' face amongst the distant waves and heard His call. She gripped the wooden side of the boat and flung her legs into the dark abyss below. Sprays of water splashed the side of her face, and her legs tried to adjust to the movement underfoot. The finer muscles in her body worked to keep her balanced, and they strained from the rolling current that sought to knock her down.

She looked out into the dark, and the face of the One she loved glowed through the black. She walked toward Him, trying not to look away, but her eyes needed to focus on her feet. She was learning to walk again by faith, and it took all of her concentration. She took several steps, scanned the night for the light, then continued further away from the boat. She couldn't look back; she knew she would fall if she did.

The light seemed to change direction several times, but it could have been the waves pushing her away. She searched for His face again and again, and she continuously altered her course. Was she going in circles? She stopped for a moment and scanned the horizon. The boat disappeared behind the shadows, and she desperately searched for the light. It was gone. She cried out, but the wind swept her voice into the void.

She felt something nudge her from within. She couldn't see it or hear it, and she wasn't sure she should trust it—but she had no choice. She allowed the pull to guide her, praying that it was Truth. Whatever it was, it was not of this world, and it was difficult to absorb its nature. However, it burned inside her; and as she followed its lead, she lifted her eyes and allowed them to search through the darkness.

She persevered with hope, but her legs began to shake from exhaustion. Her arms grew tired from grasping through air. And her eyes strained from sifting through the emptiness. She could no longer walk; she wanted to relax her body and slip into the sea. The current seemed inviting, willing her to stay idle in its caress. But the prompting in her spirit intensified, and it compelled her forward. Eyes closed and body fighting to continue, she allowed the Spirit in her to guide her.

Suddenly, she felt excitement swell in her chest. She opened her eyes and saw Him—Jesus! She pushed her legs and ran, gaining momentum as her arms sliced through the wind. Unblinking, her gaze stayed on His face. She wouldn't lose Him this time. The waves blocked her view, but only for a moment. The Spirit inside of her willed her onward and while her feet kicked, water sprinkled around her like rain.

Jesus reached out for her, and she dove toward Him, clasping her arms around His ankles. The lower half of her body sunk into water, but she kept her chin above the current, holding tightly to her Savior. She made it; she was safe. She could stay at His feet forever and be content. She rested and allowed her body to sway with the water. After a time, she felt Jesus move His feet, so she looked up.

"Get up, my daughter," He said.

"I can't, Jesus. I gave You all I had trying to get here. There's nothing left in me. I'm done."

"There's a well-spring inside of you. Get up, and I'll show you."

The woman held on to Jesus' feet for a moment longer. He expected too much. It was a miracle she had gotten this far. She would get up and show Him her weakness. She let go of His feet and gripped the current. She pulled herself onto her knees and felt the waves spiral beneath her. Jesus reached down His hand and lifted her to a stance. Her legs mimicked the flow, and her body balanced to the rhythm of the sea. Jesus let go of her hand, and she felt secure by His side.

"This is easy, Jesus! I'm standing as If I were on solid ground!" she exclaimed.

Jesus smiled. "You are on solid ground."

"What do we do next?" she asked.

"Follow me," Jesus answered, and He lunged back and sprang into the air.

The woman watched Jesus fly into the midnight sky. She felt the pull inside of her beckon her to Him.

"I can't fly!" she yelled out.

"I will teach you," she heard. "You will learn by faith. I have a life not bound by limits prepared for you. Will you trust me?"

She looked down at the water and moved her legs confidently with the tide. Walking on water was no longer a challenge. She looked back up and saw the glow of Jesus skimming the air. She knew learning to fly would be harder than she could imagine, but excitement filled her spirit with anticipation. It would be worth the sacrifice. She stepped back and dug her toes into the water. She directed her eyes toward the sky and prepared her muscles for the leap.

"Tell me to fly with You, and I will," she whispered.

"Fly with Me!"

The woman jumped with all her strength.

The Final Show

I imagine myself as a frail, old woman. It is dusk, and I'm walking outside down the street with strangers. I have nothing left of value. My money has been passed along to my kids and God's service. My youth and beauty have died long ago. My body is broken, and my five senses have faded. My mind is forgetful, and I can't keep a schedule. I can barely muster the energy to complete the daily tasks of living. I live each day longing for my Love's return.

I hear a scream, and see people running away in fear. I look to the heavens just in time to see the star sprinkled night sky rip in half. The black drape ripples like a blanket and falls on either side of the earth. All around me is the absence of darkness. I could have never comprehended such light.

I feel the earth flatten and draw together; all the peoples of the earth now have a front row seat to the final show. From the sky's center stage, a Man appears riding a winged horse. An expanse of angels stretch for miles to His left and right. The Man wears many crowns, and on his thigh is written, "KING OF KINGS AND LORD OF LORDS." His face is blazing fire, and His strength vibrates the earth.

I fall to my knees and stare at the majesty of my Love. "Beautiful," I whisper. "More beautiful than I could ever imagine."

I offer my last confession: "Forgive me, Father. I did not describe Your beauty adequately with my words. I fell short of emulating Your glory with my life."

Around me a few people linger. They are the children of the Most High, and the Spirit of God in them affirms the time. They fall to their knees in despair. A man next to me pulls money out of his pockets, sacrificing it willingly. A woman in front of me eagerly offers up her beauty. Prestige, careers, children, fame, schedules, pleasures and worry are laid out on the footstool of the King, but it is too late. God had asked for their sacrifices, but they ignored His requests.

Thunderous praise steals my gaze back to the horizon, and my Love eases His horse onto the earth. He has returned, and my heart is overwhelmed with joy. Yet...I have nothing left to offer Him. During my life, I gave Him everything He asked of me. He requested each thing I held dear—my mind, my husband, my children, my career, my dreams, my time, my money—and piece by piece, I handed my life over to His will.

I look to my Love. Would He remember that I gave Him all I had? Did I hear the Spirit's leading correctly? Have I lived the life that He desired for me? Does He know how much I love Him? The King walks toward me; His confidence causes the air around Him to shake. I open my aged arms wide. They are empty. I am empty. There is nothing left. "Jesus, I am unworthy," I whisper. "But I love You. I love You. I love You." I can say no more.

Jesus gets on His knee before me, and He strokes the side of my wrinkled face. His smile radiates light, and His tears shimmer down His cheek.

He looks into my eyes and says, "I loved you first." He fills my empty arms with His glory, and my crumpled, old skin falls to the ground. The old is gone. I am new in Christ.

"Therefore, if anyone is in Christ, the new creation has come: The old has gone, the new is here!" (2 Corinthians 5.17 NIV).

The Great Egret

I saw a Great Egret clinging to
A wood post one dismal day.
His white feathers shown bright
Against the grey and gloomy bay.

The wind circled around the pillar,
Taunting the Egret to sway.
But he stood stony silent,
Moving neither way.

The rain prodded the quiet Egret,
But not a feather did he stray.
I wondered why in a fierce squall
The Egret's flight would delay.

God whispered, "Stand strong the storm,
And my Glory I will display."
The sun squelched that vexing gale,
And the Egret soared away.

Hope's Toll

Forsaken in my circumstance
Left idle on the floor
Jumped to another second chance
That ended like before

But my God is faithful
His love steadfast
My trust outweighs the hurt
And Hope will last

Doubt dares to distort my vision
Fear yearns to tear my strength
Hold the noose of indecision
Like a snake at arm's length

But my God is faithful
His love steadfast
My trust outweighs the hurt
And Hope will last

Let go of my understanding
Patient heart on Your throne
My desires cease demanding

Loyalty I have sown

How my God is faithful
His love steadfast
My trust outweighs the hurt
And Hope will last

Peace seeps into tight constriction
Joy sings a freedom song
Christ bestows a benediction
Embracing all my wrong

My faith saves my steps
God's love heals the soul
Trust outweighs my hurt
And Hope takes her toll

I pray you enjoyed this collection of meditations. I would be honored if you would write a review on Amazon. You can find my other fiction and non-fiction books at Amazon or on my blog, www.alisahopewagner.com.

www.ingramcontent.com/pod-product-compliance
Lightning Source LLC
LaVergne TN
LVHW051230080426
835513LV00016B/1502